Food

Cut the Fruit

GOOD JOB!

If you cut each fruit along the dotted line, what would it look like inside?
Draw a line from ● to ● to connect each fruit to its cross section.

To Parents Children's scientific thinking is developed through close observation of the things around them.

apple

orange

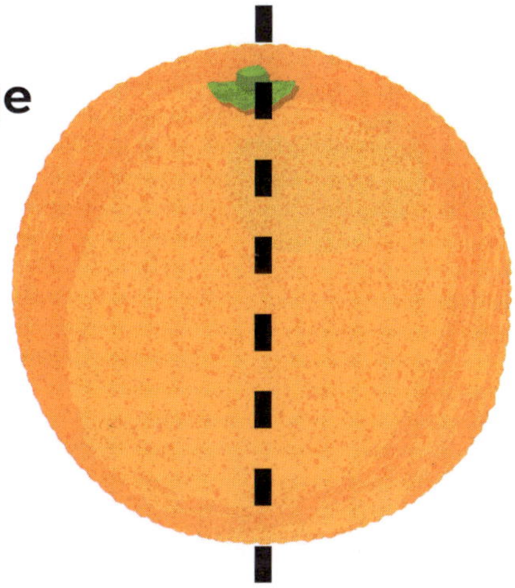

apricot

Place the Seed Stickers

Put a seed sticker on each fruit.

GOOD JOB!

To Parents When looking at fruit, pay attention to the seeds. The size, number, and position of the seeds depend on the fruit.

apple

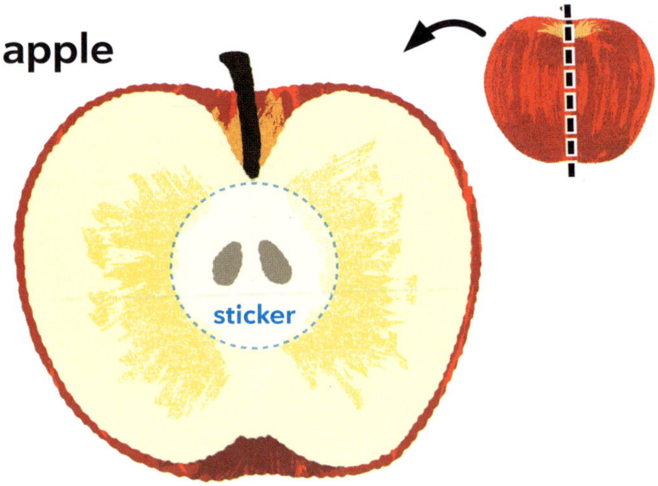

sticker

kiwifruit

sticker

cherry

sticker

apricot

sticker

lemon

sticker

Food

Cut the Fruit

If you cut each fruit along the dotted line, what would it look like inside?
Draw a line from ● to ● to connect each fruit to its cross section.

To Parents Cut fruits horizontally with your child, instead of cutting them vertically like you normally would.

apple

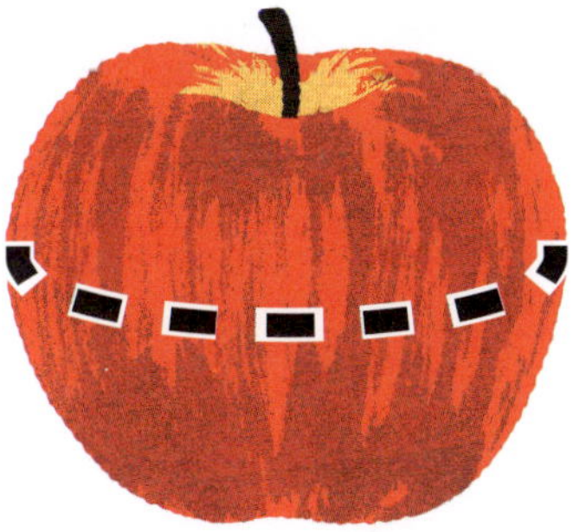

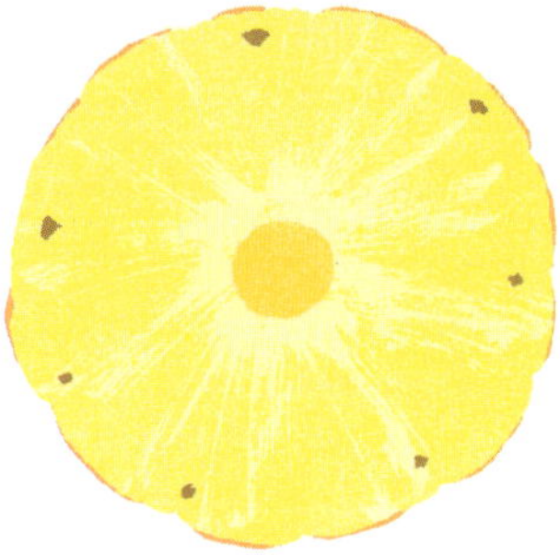

orange

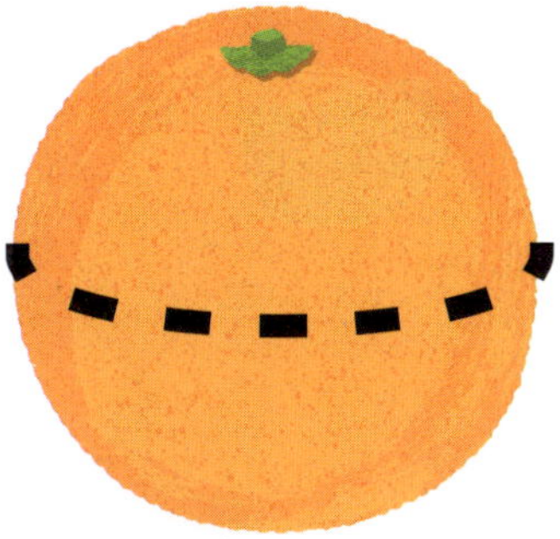

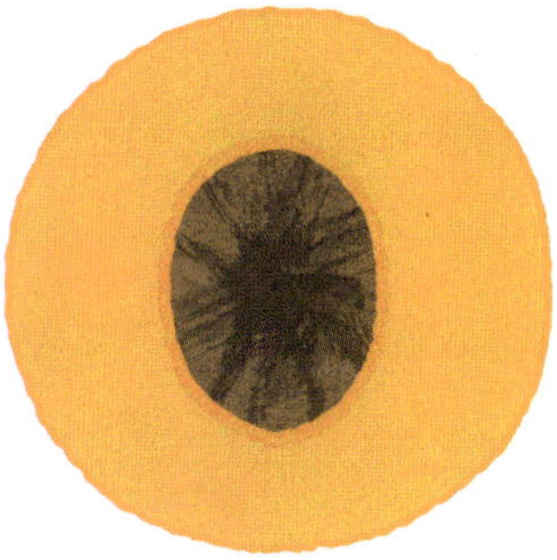

apricot

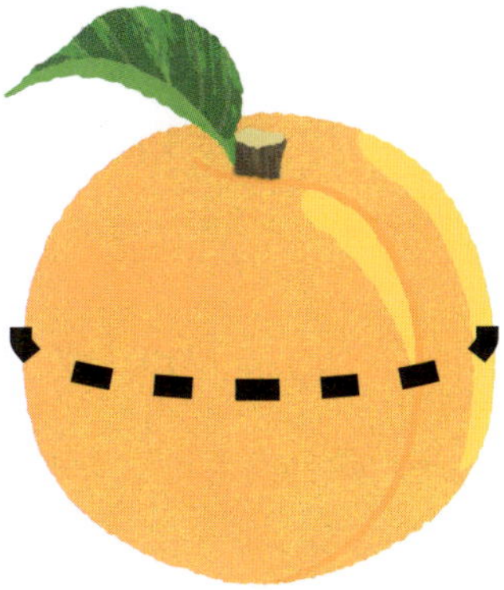

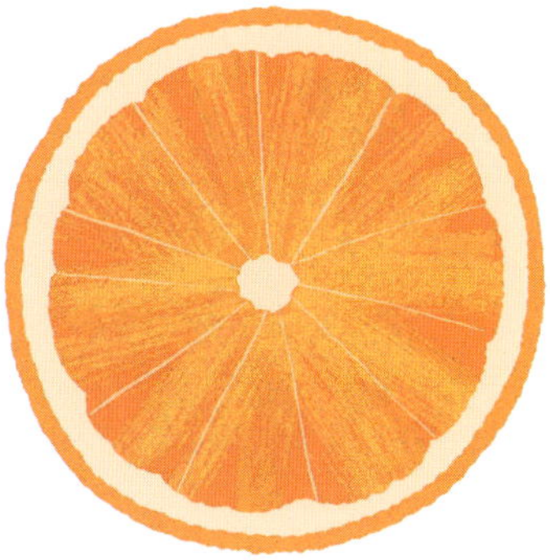

pineapple

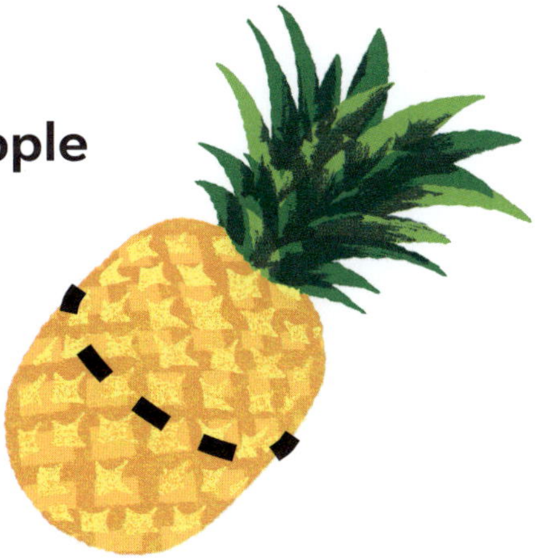

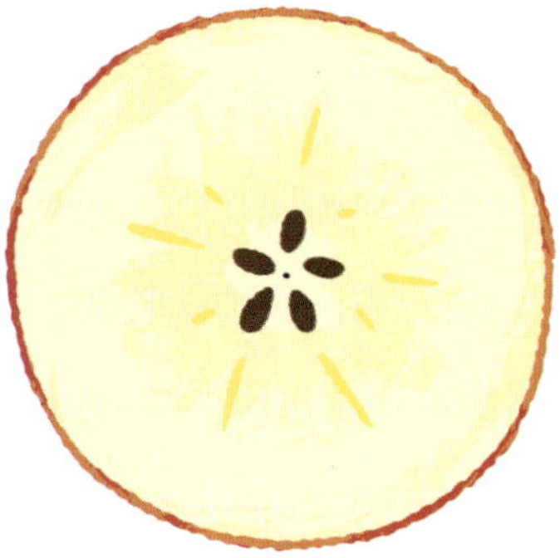

Food

Cut the Fruit

If you cut each fruit along the dotted line, what would it look like inside?
Draw a line from ● to ● to connect each fruit to its cross section.

To Parents The small black dots on bananas are seed traces. The small grains on the outside of a strawberry are actually the fruit. The red part is called the receptacle, which is the swollen base of the flower.

kiwifruit

banana

cantaloupe

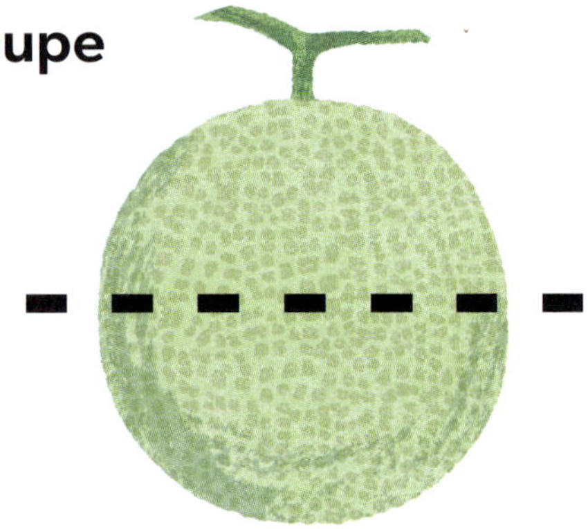

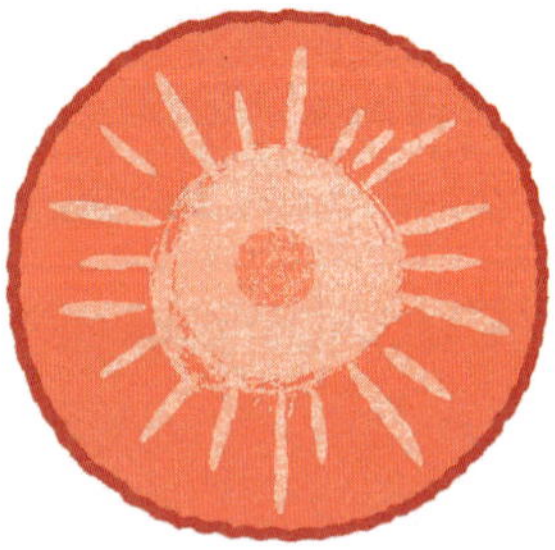

strawberry

Food

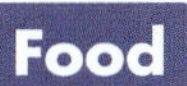

Cut the Fruit

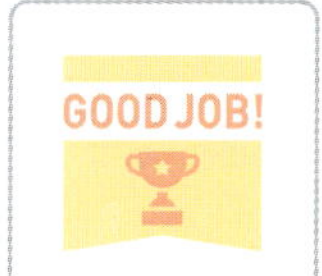

If you cut each fruit along the dotted line, what would it look like inside?
Find the correct picture, and draw a ○ in the □ next to it.

watermelon

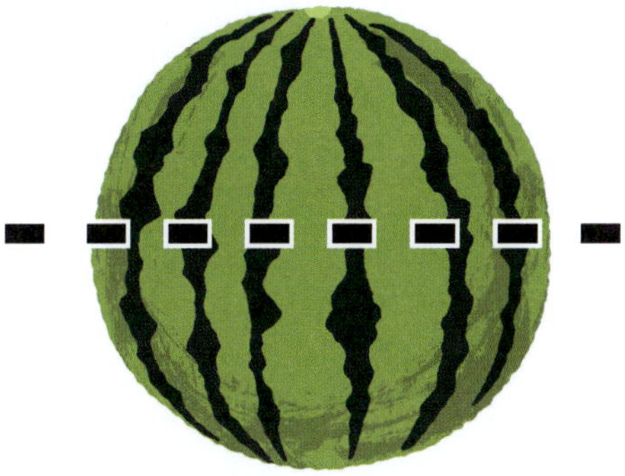

□ 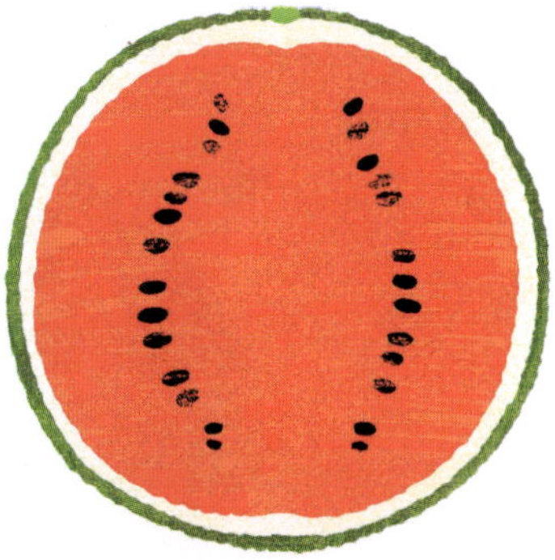

□ 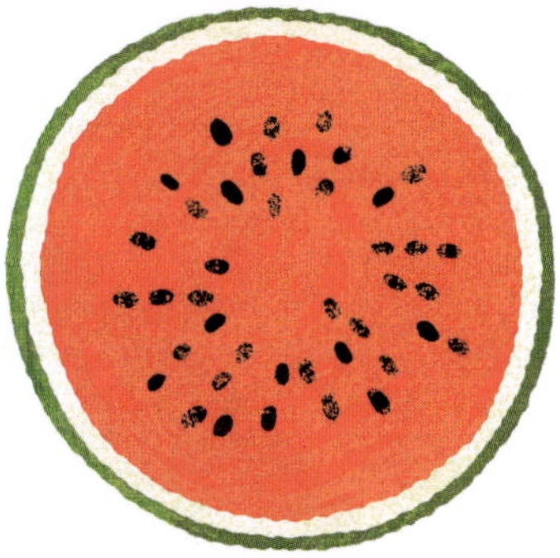

cantaloupe

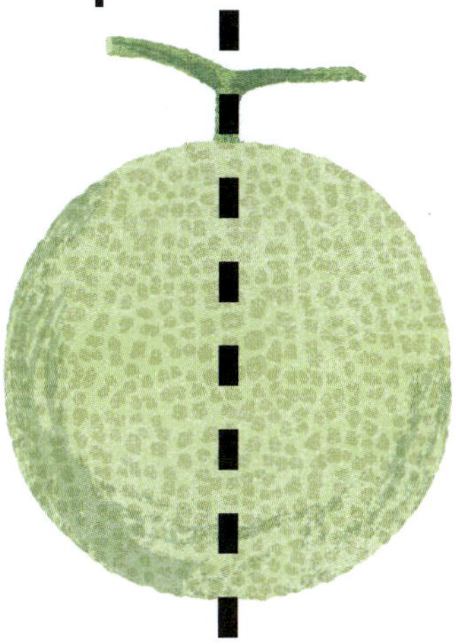

□ 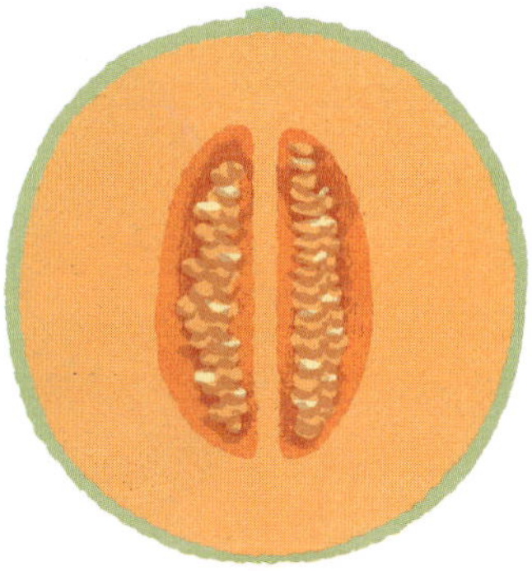

□ 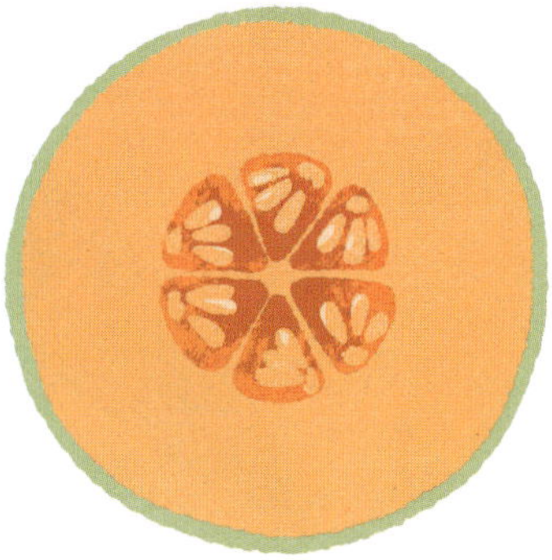

Cut the Produce

If you cut each vegetable along the dotted line, what would it look like inside? Draw a line from ● to ● to connect each vegetable to its cross section.

eggplant

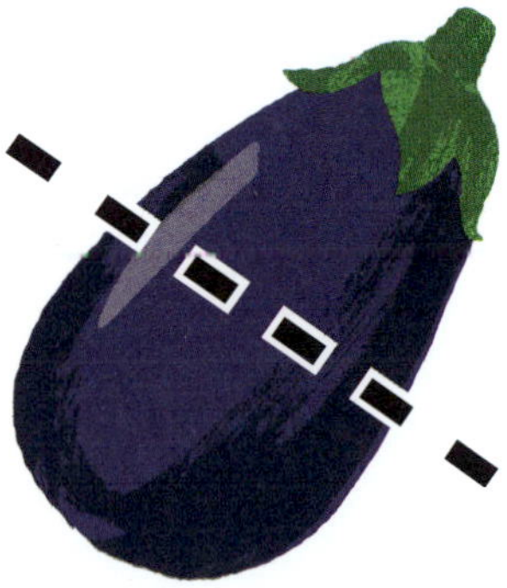

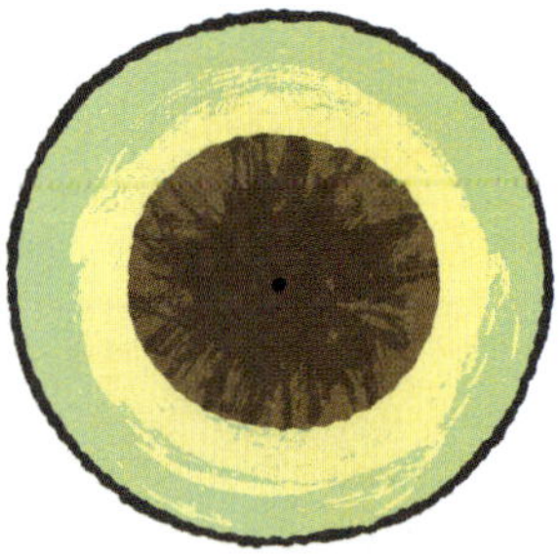

cucumber

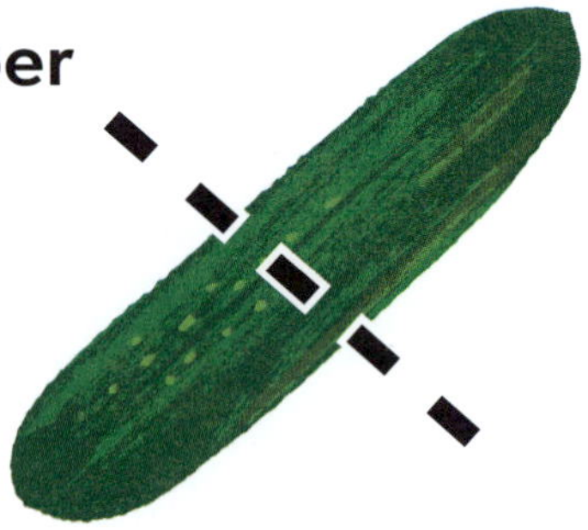

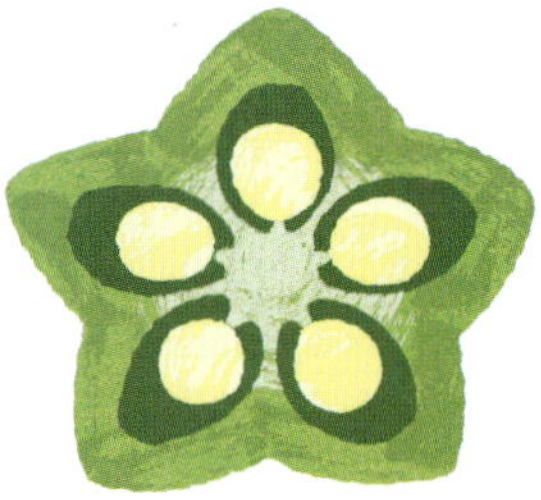

avocado

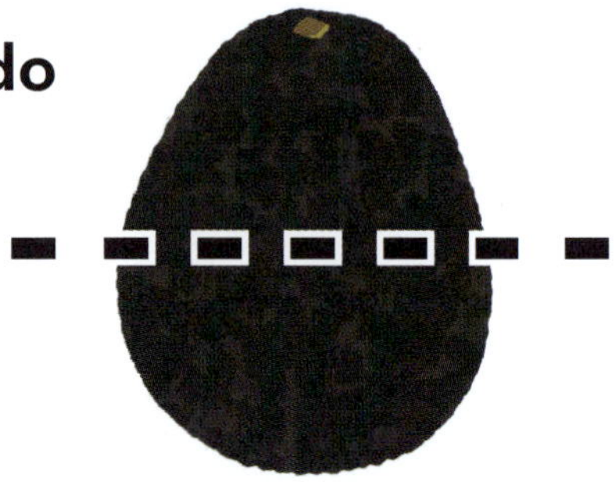

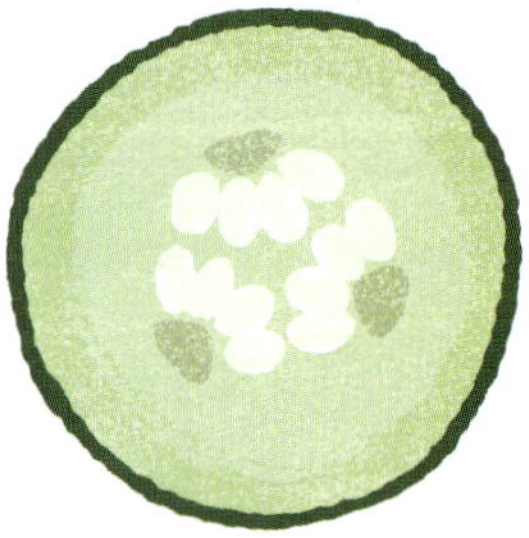

okra

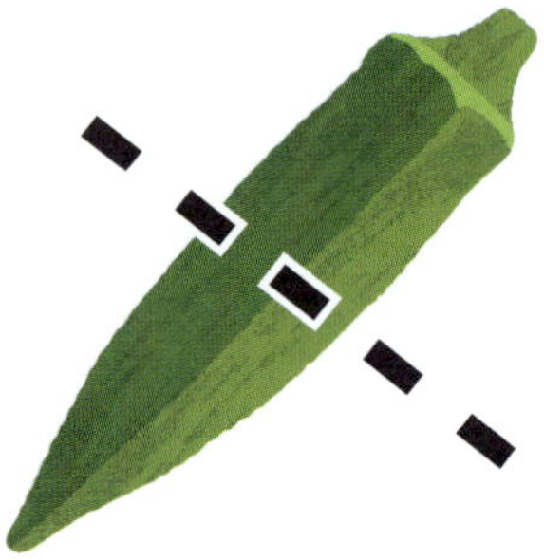

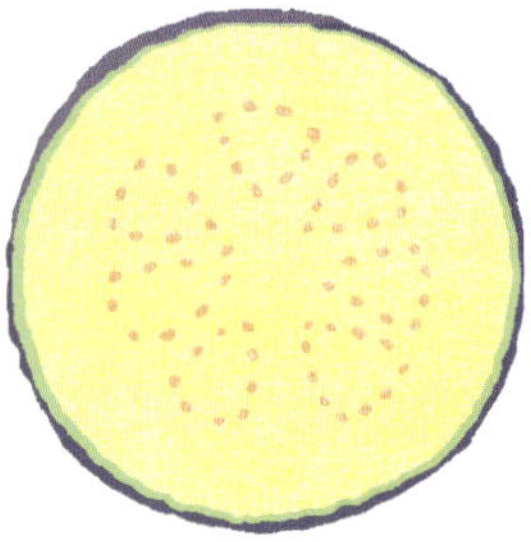

Cut the Vegetables

If you cut each vegetable along the dotted line, what would it look like inside? Find the correct picture, and draw a ◯ in the □ next to it.

tomato

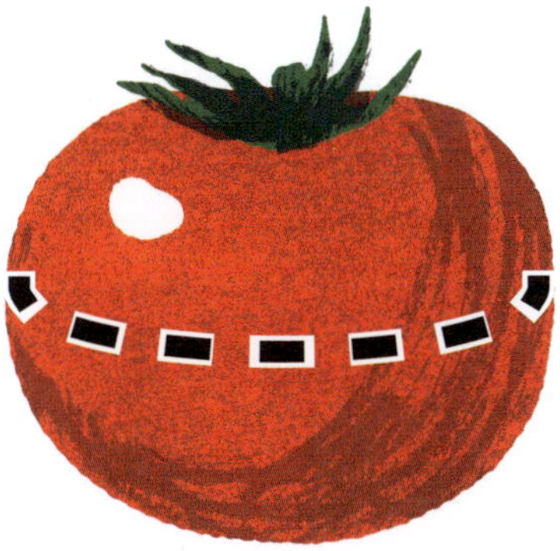

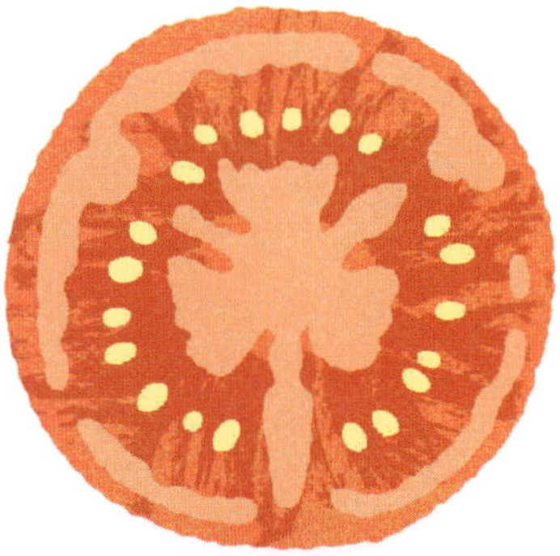

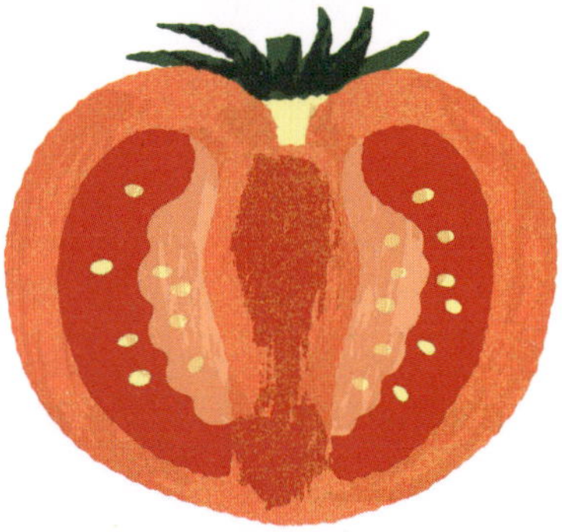

□

□

cabbage

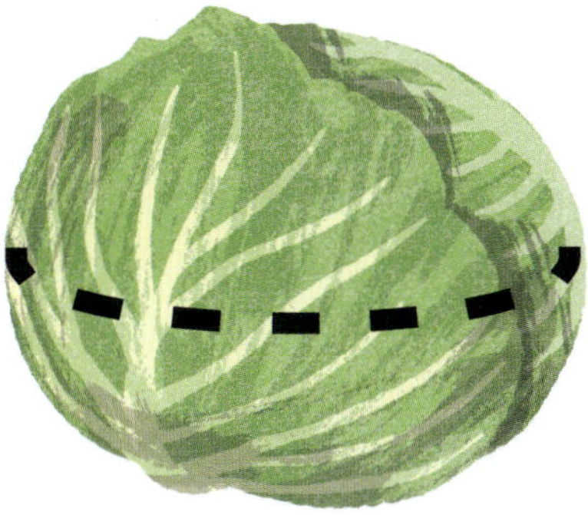

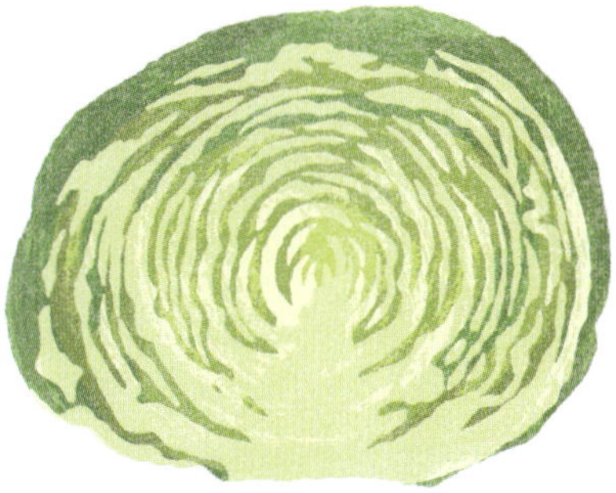

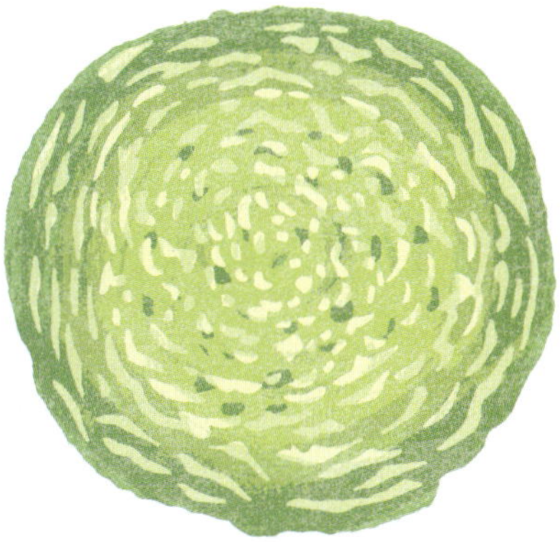

□

□

Food

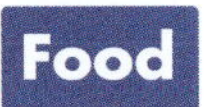

Match the Plant Parts

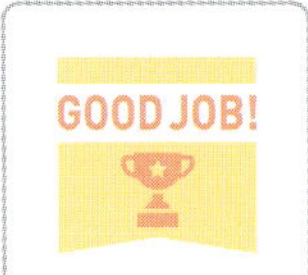

Draw a line from ● to ● to connect each food to its seed or grain.

corn

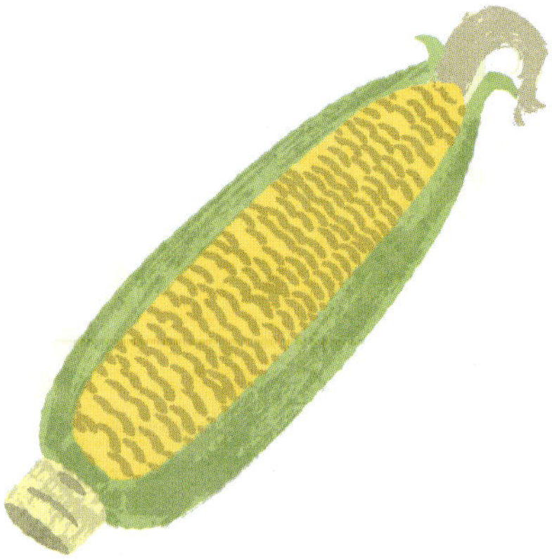

● ●

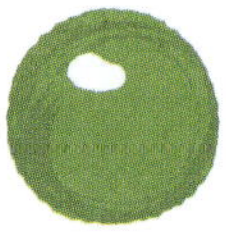

pea

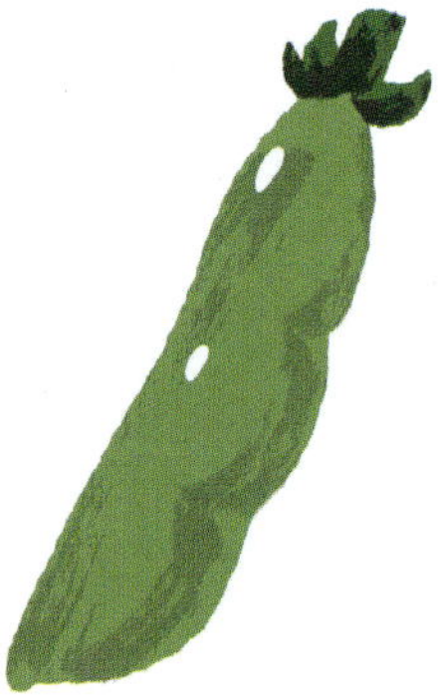

● ●

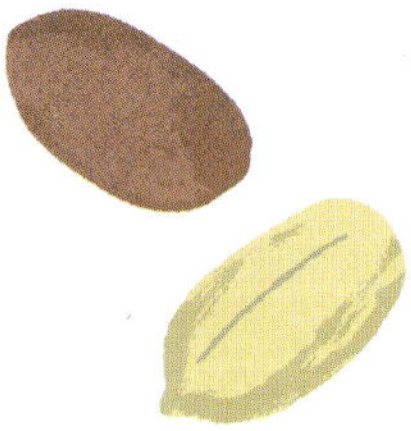

peanut

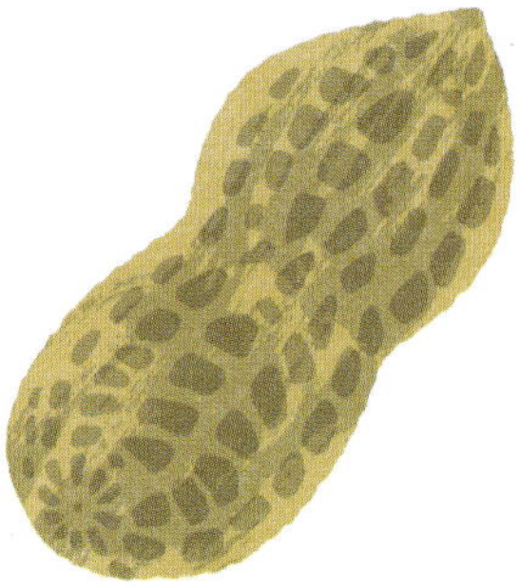

● ●

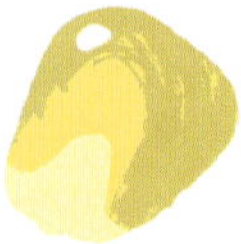

Place the Seed Stickers

Put a seed sticker near the matching flower.

To Parents Germination requires air, water, and a particular range of temperature. Avoid planting seeds too deep in the soil and covering them with too much soil.

sunflower

sticker

morning glory

sticker

tomato

sticker

rose

sticker

Plants

Write the Numbers in Order

Write the numbers 1 to 4 in the ☐ in the order in which the strawberry grows.

To Parents Insects visit strawberry plants and help move pollen from the plant's stamen to its pistil. Then strawberries begin to grow.

Plants

Match the Leaf to the Flower

Draw a line from ● to ● to connect each leaf to its flower.

To Parents Leaf shape varies from plant to plant. Pay attention to the leaves as well as the flowers.

dandelion

tulip

carnation

sunflower

Plants

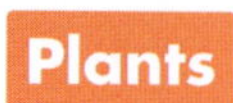

Match the Leaf to the Flower

Draw a line from ● to ● to connect each leaf to its flower.

rose clover

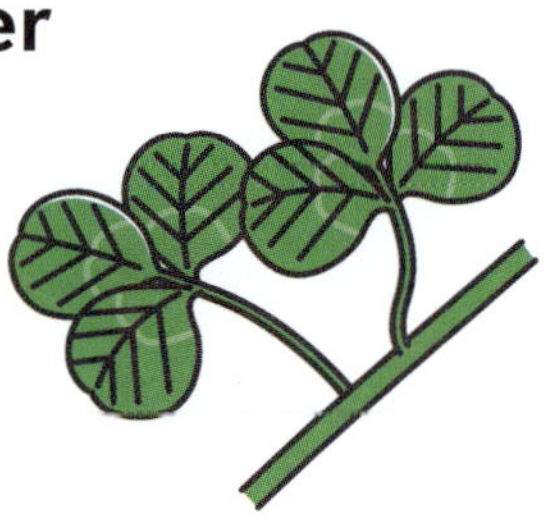

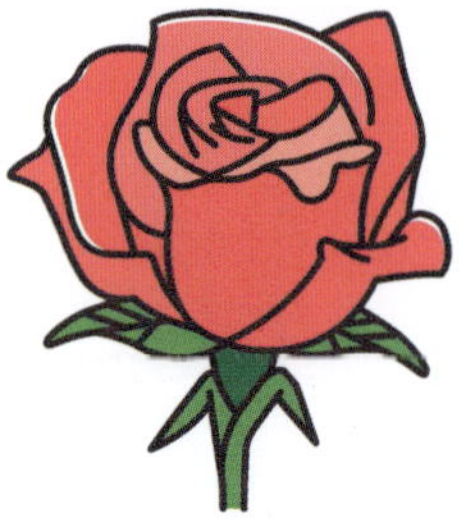

rose

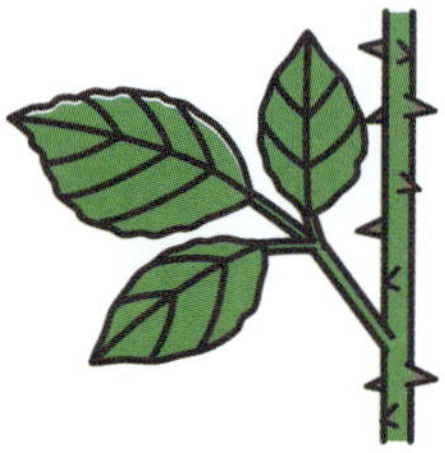

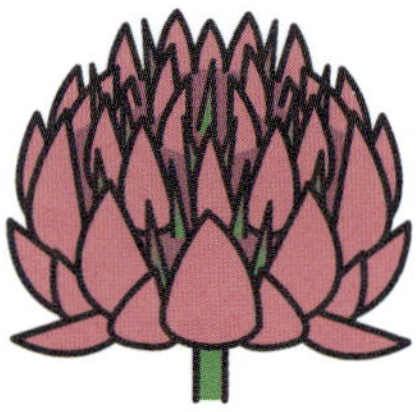

daisy

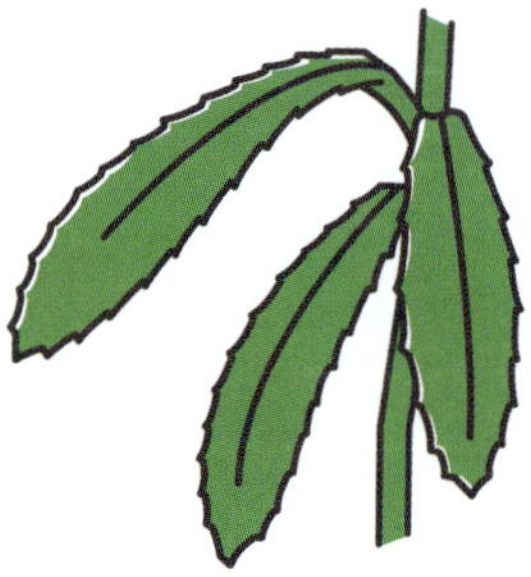

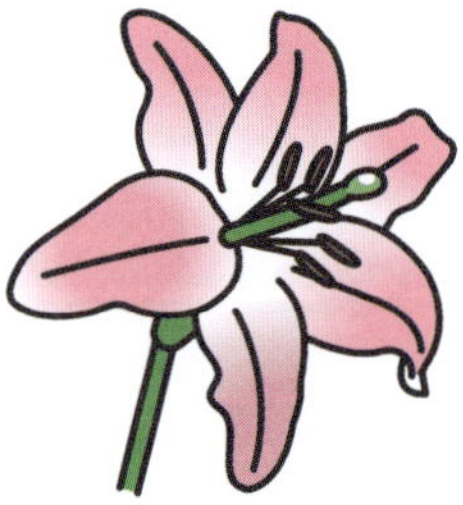

lily

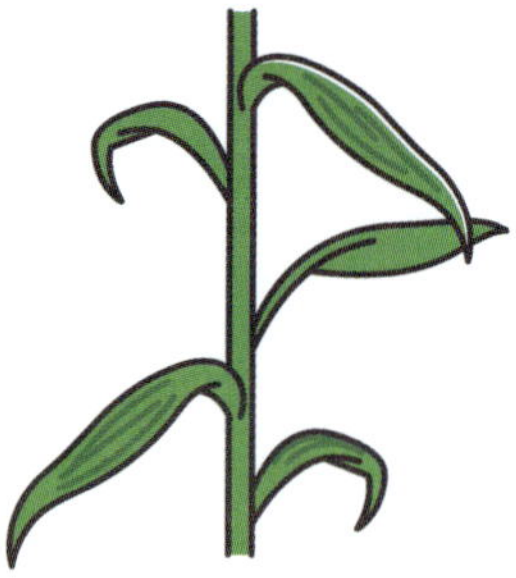

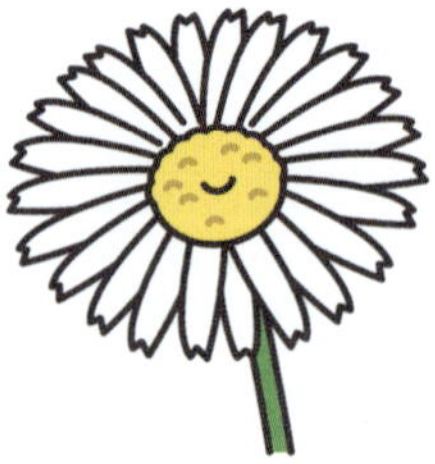

Place the Petal Stickers

GOOD JOB!

Put petal stickers on each flower.

To Parents A lily appears to have six petals, but three of them are true petals and the other three are sepals. Sepals look like petals but are tougher. They help protect the flower bud before it opens.

Match the Flower to Its Vegetable

Put the flower stickers on the matching vegetable plants.

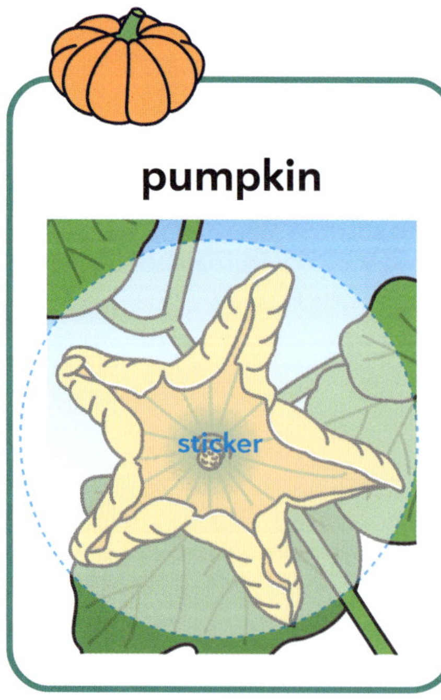

Plants

Which Part of the Plant Do We Eat?

Edible vegetables grow in different parts of the plant.
Put the vegetable stickers in the group where they belong.

Some vegetables are the leafy parts of a plant.

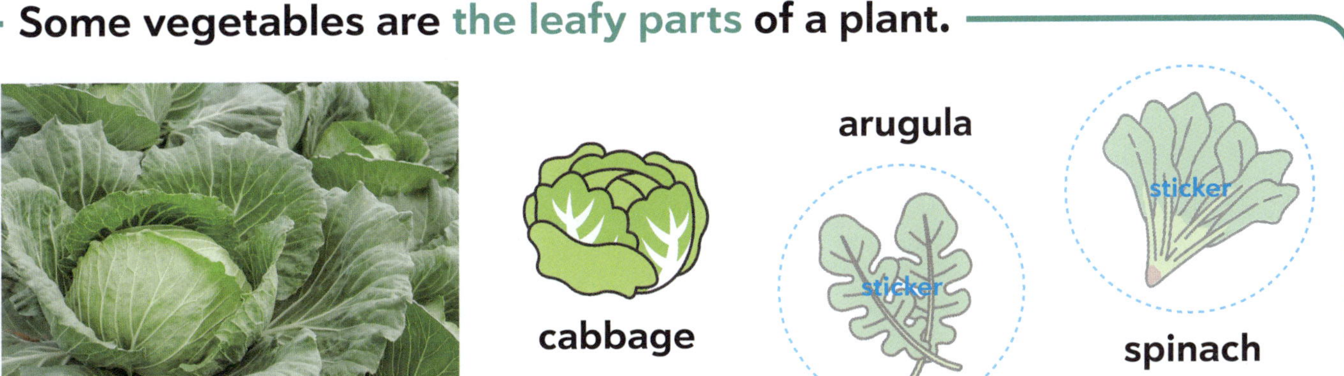

Some vegetables are the root part of a plant.

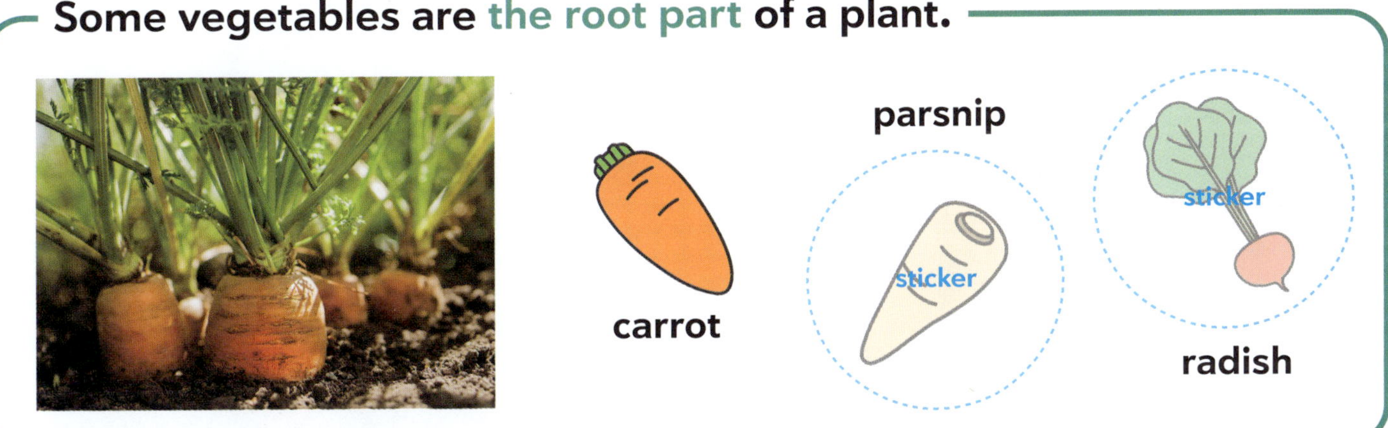

Some vegetables are the flower part of a plant.

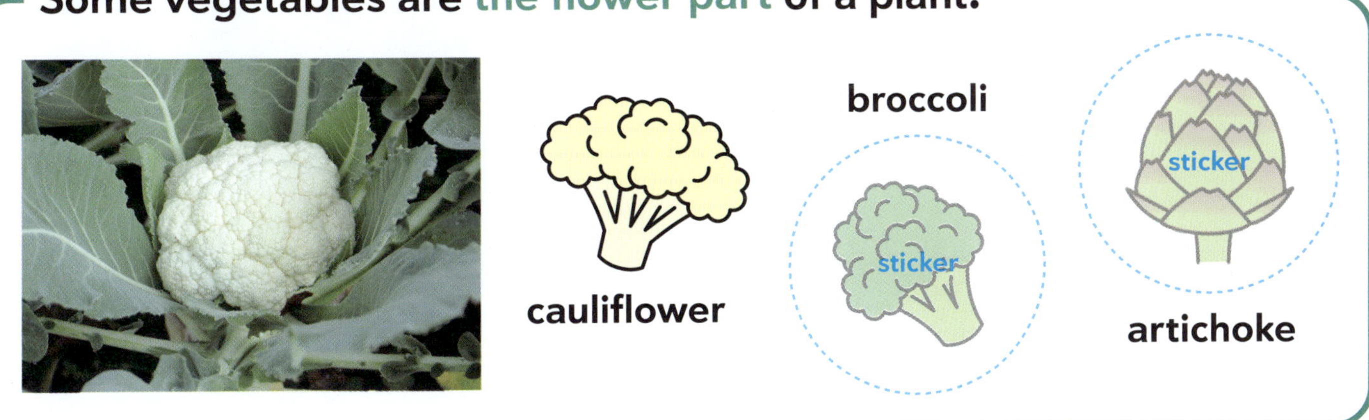

Write the Numbers in Order

The dogwood changes with the seasons. Write the numbers 1 to 4 in the □ in the order of spring → summer → autumn → winter.

Animals

Match the Creature to Their Habitat

Draw a line from ● to ● to connect each creature to the place where they live.

To Parents Animals live where the food they eat exists. The oriental longheaded locust eats grass plants and lives in sunny meadows. Beavers prefer to eat leaves, bark, twigs, and aquatic plants.

beaver

octopus

black-capped chickadee

oriental longheaded locust

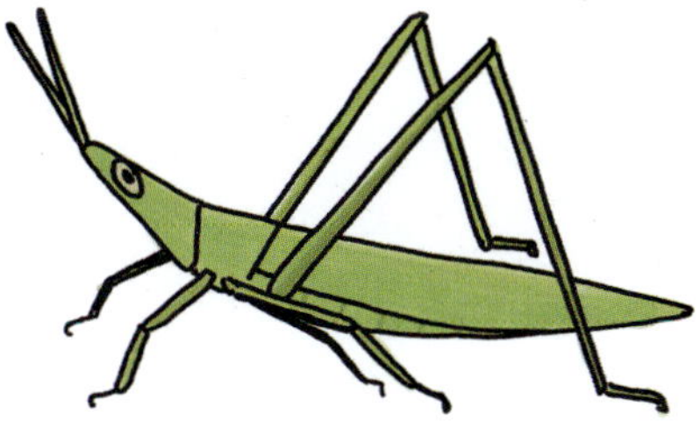

sea

grassy field

lake

woods

What Doesn't Live in the Sea?

Find two creatures that do not live in the sea, and draw an X in the ( ) below them.

To Parents Most amphibians, such as frogs and salamanders, live in freshwater because their skin has to stay moist so they can breathe. They lose moisture from their bodies in a highly saline environment such as seawater.

starfish
( )

squid
( )

salmon
( )

salamander
( )

crab
( )

sea urchin
( )

sea anemone
( )

frog
( )

Find the Birds

Find the birds and draw a ◯ in the (   ) next to each one.

To Parents Bats are the only mammals that fly. They fly using a thin membrane of skin between their fingers and long forepaws. Flying squirrels, also mammals, glide using flight membranes that run from their sides to the base of their tail.

owl (   )

bat (   )

penguin (   )

flying squirrel (   )

chicken (   )

ostrich (   )

Find the Fish

Find the fish and draw a ○ in the ( ) next to each one.

To Parents Dolphins and whales are mammals. The females give birth to babies and breastfeed them. Flying fish are fish. Their pectoral fins have evolved to look like wings.

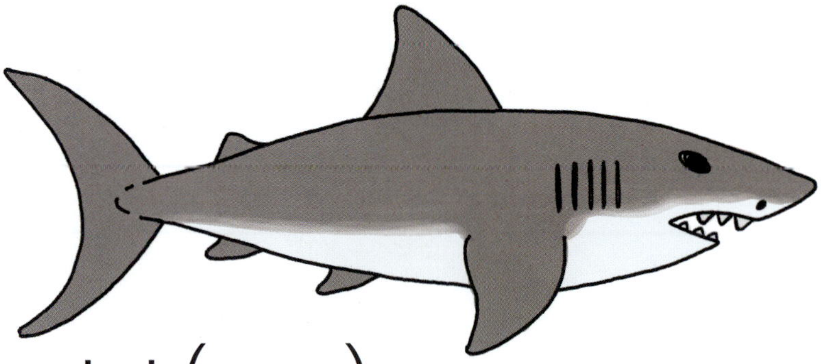

flying fish (   )

shark (   )

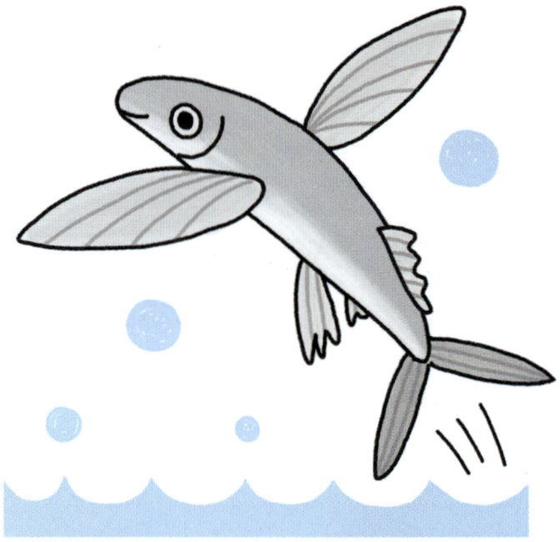

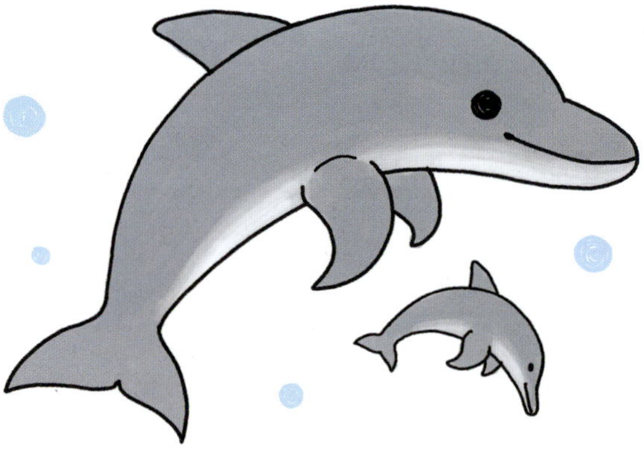

dolphins (   )

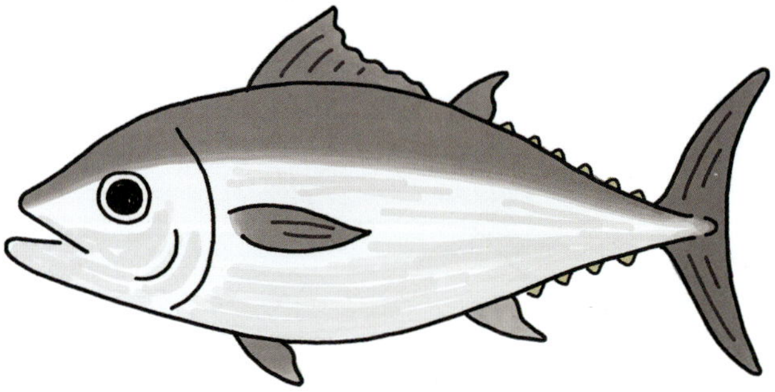

tuna (   )

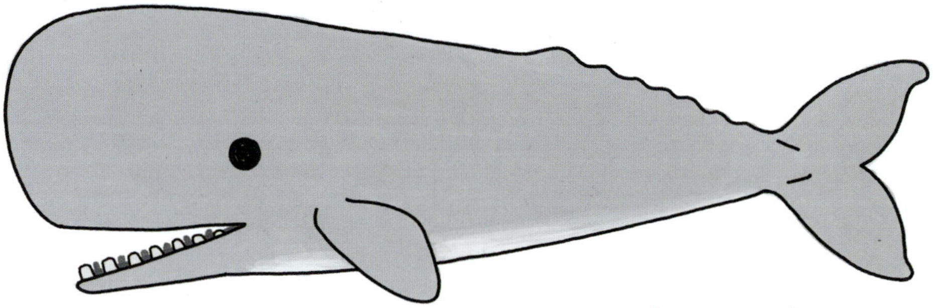

whale (   )

Match the Animal to Its Foot

Draw a line from ● to ● to connect each creature to its foot.

To Parents Frogs and rabbits have well-developed hind legs for jumping. Most frogs have webbed feet. The sea lion's flippers are better suited to swimming in the sea than to life on land. Monkeys have legs that enable them to grip tree branches tightly.

frog ?

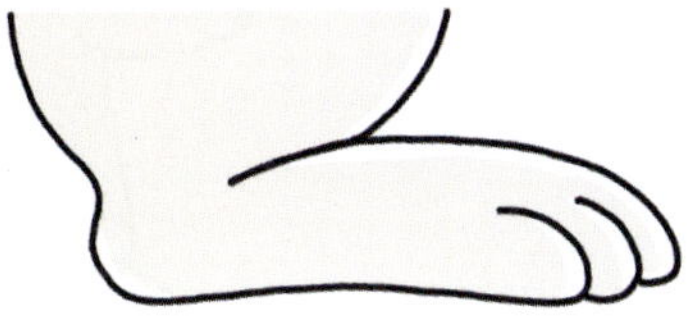

rabbit ?

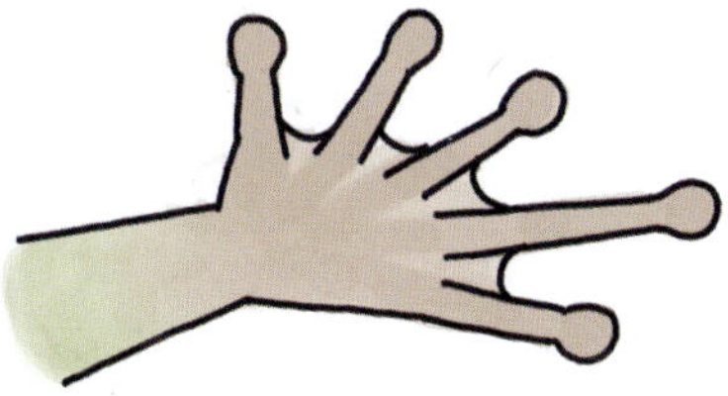

sea lion ?

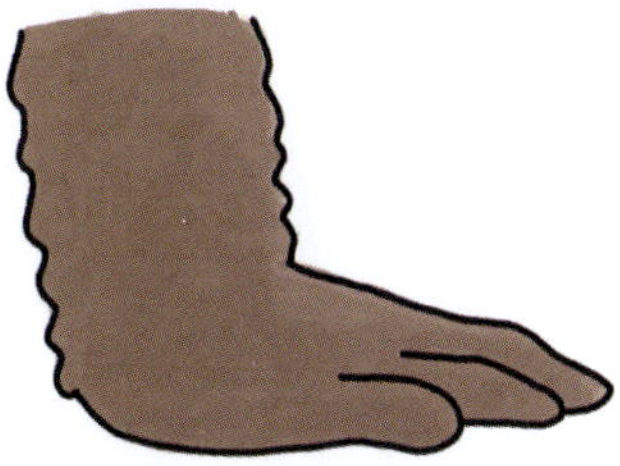

monkey ?

Match the Animal to Its Foot

Draw a line from ● to ● to connect each creature to its foot.

To Parents Kangaroos have well-developed hind legs for jumping and moving around. Elephants have sturdy legs to support their large bodies.

kangaroo

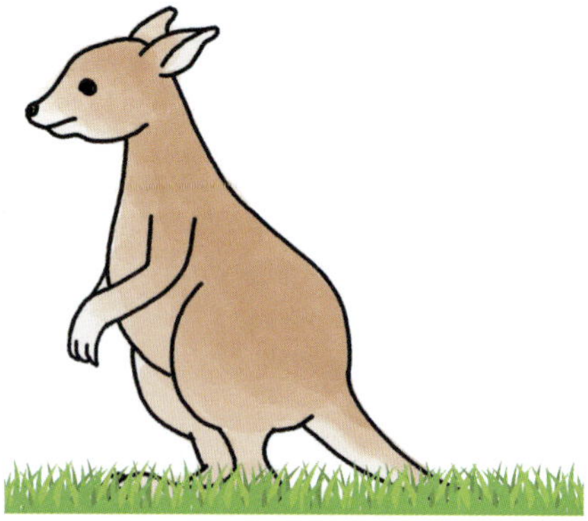

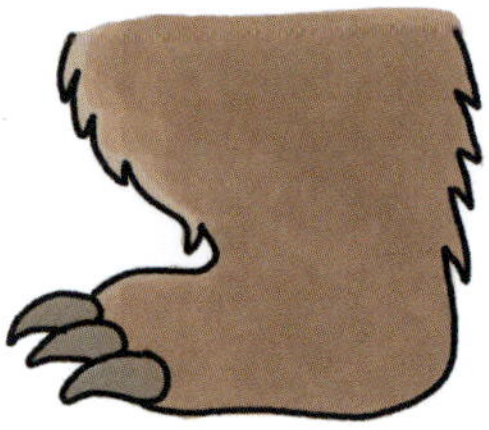

bear

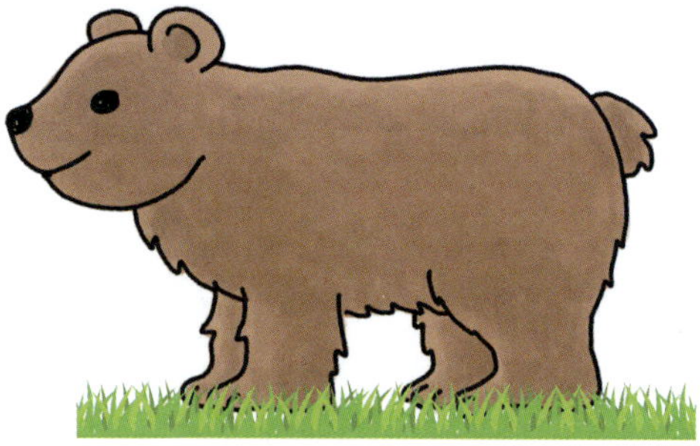

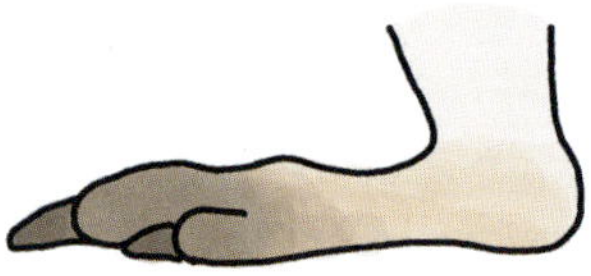

elephant

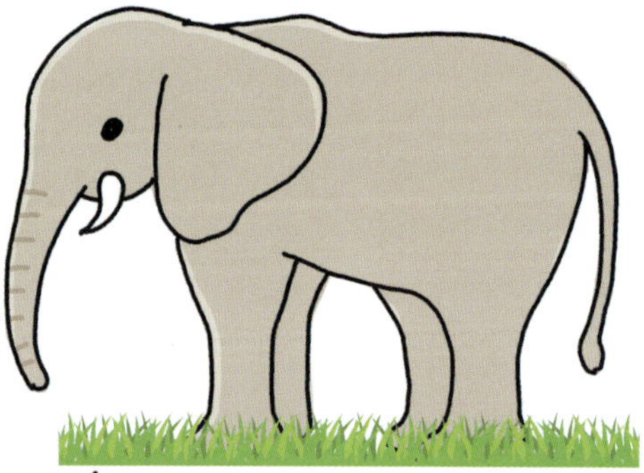

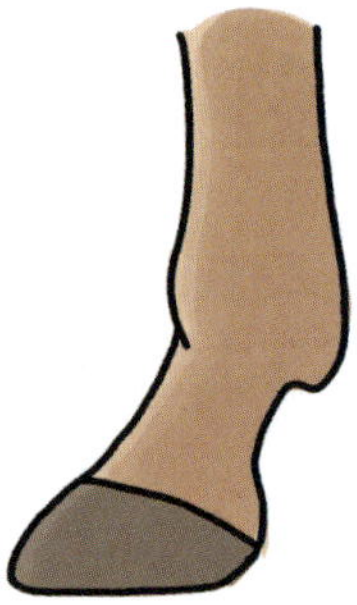

horse

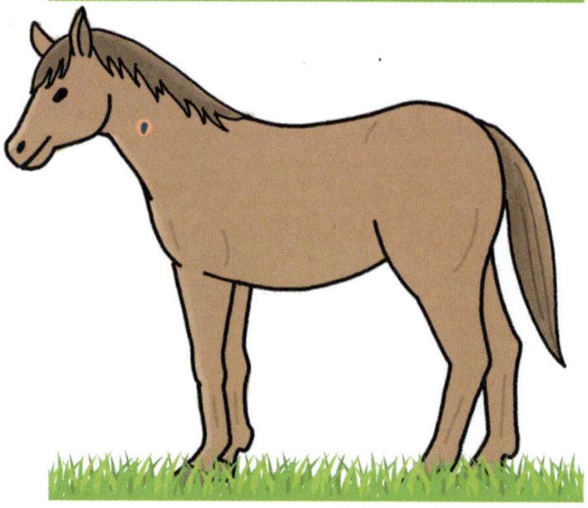

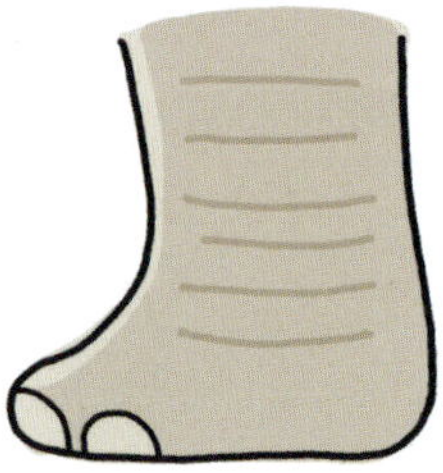

Animals

Match the Animal to Its Ears

Put the ear stickers on the animals.

To Parents Rabbits' long ears help them hear better and lose body heat in hot weather. The small ears of polar bears, which live in colder areas, lose less body heat and help them stay warm in cold weather.

sticker sticker

panda

sticker sticker

polar bear

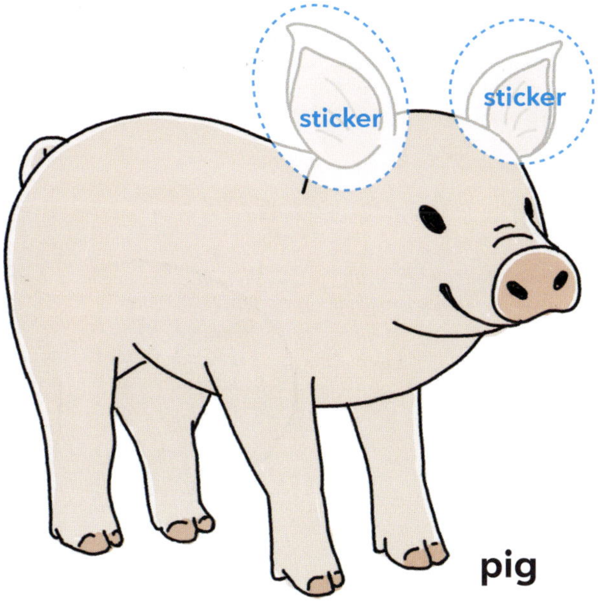

sticker sticker

pig

sticker

rabbit

Match the Animal to Its Ears

Draw a line from ● to ● to connect each animal to its ears.

To Parents Cupping your hands behind your ears makes it easier to hear sounds. Similarly, animals with large ears are better at collecting and hearing quiet sounds.

koala

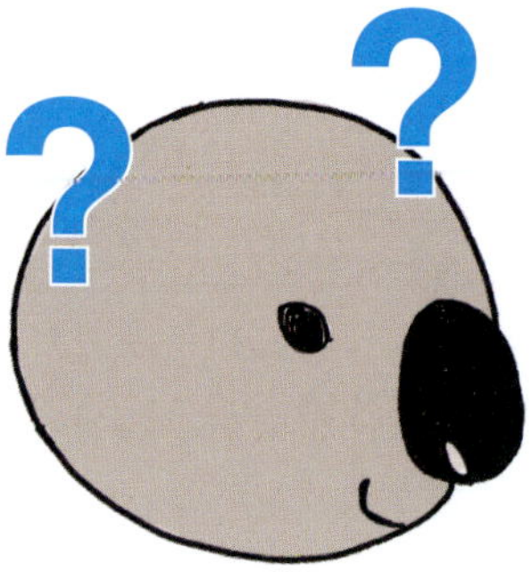

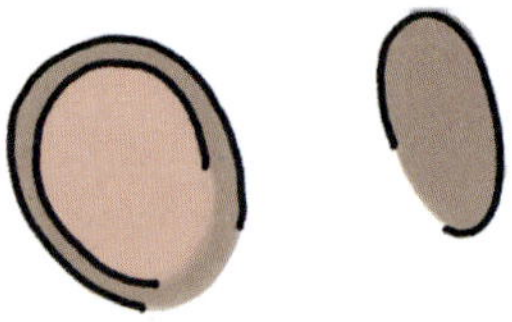

elephant

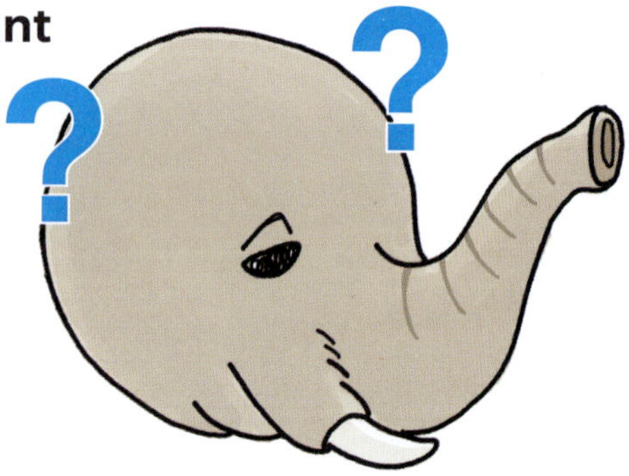

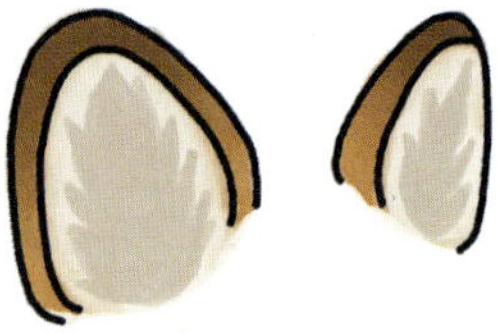

fox

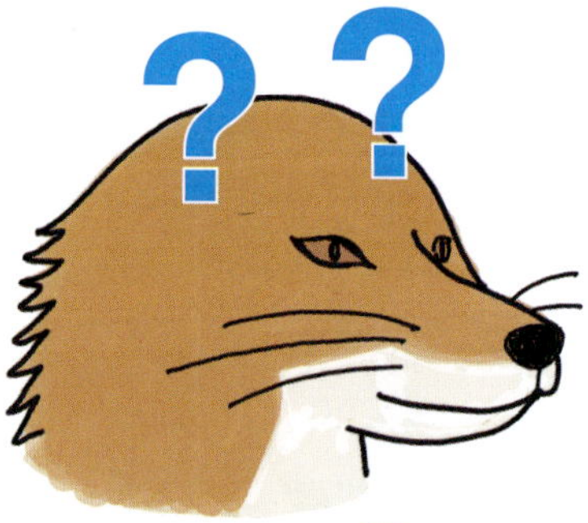

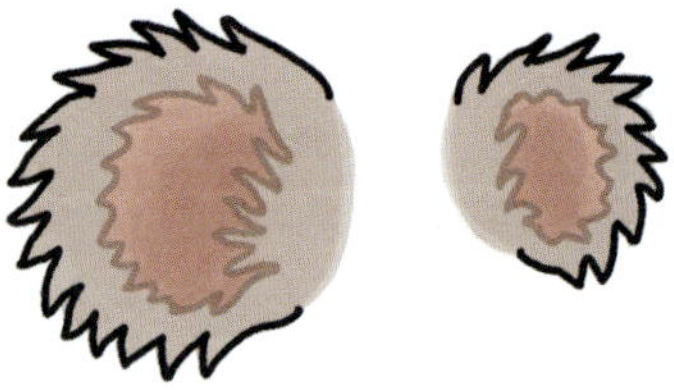

mouse

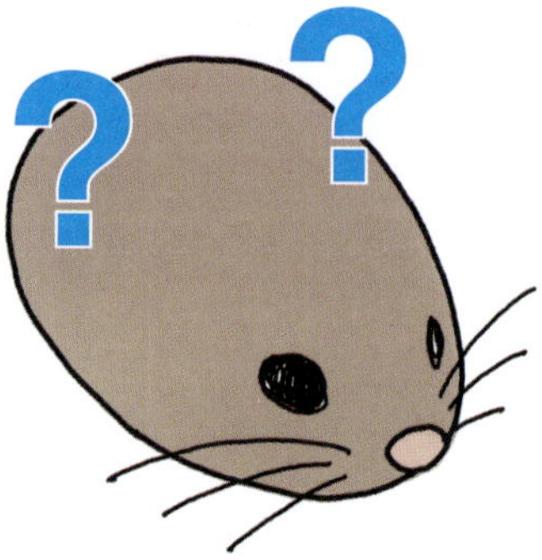

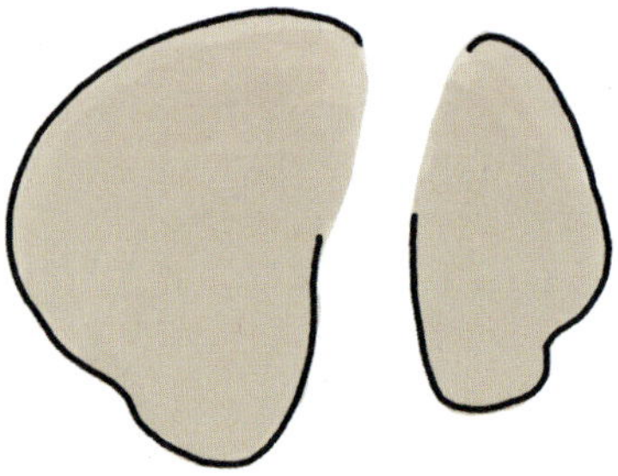

Match the Animal to Its Tail

Draw a line from ● to ● to connect each animal to its tail.

To Parents The tails of horses and cows help them ward off flies and horseflies. A fox's large tail helps it balance its body when running and making sudden changes of direction.

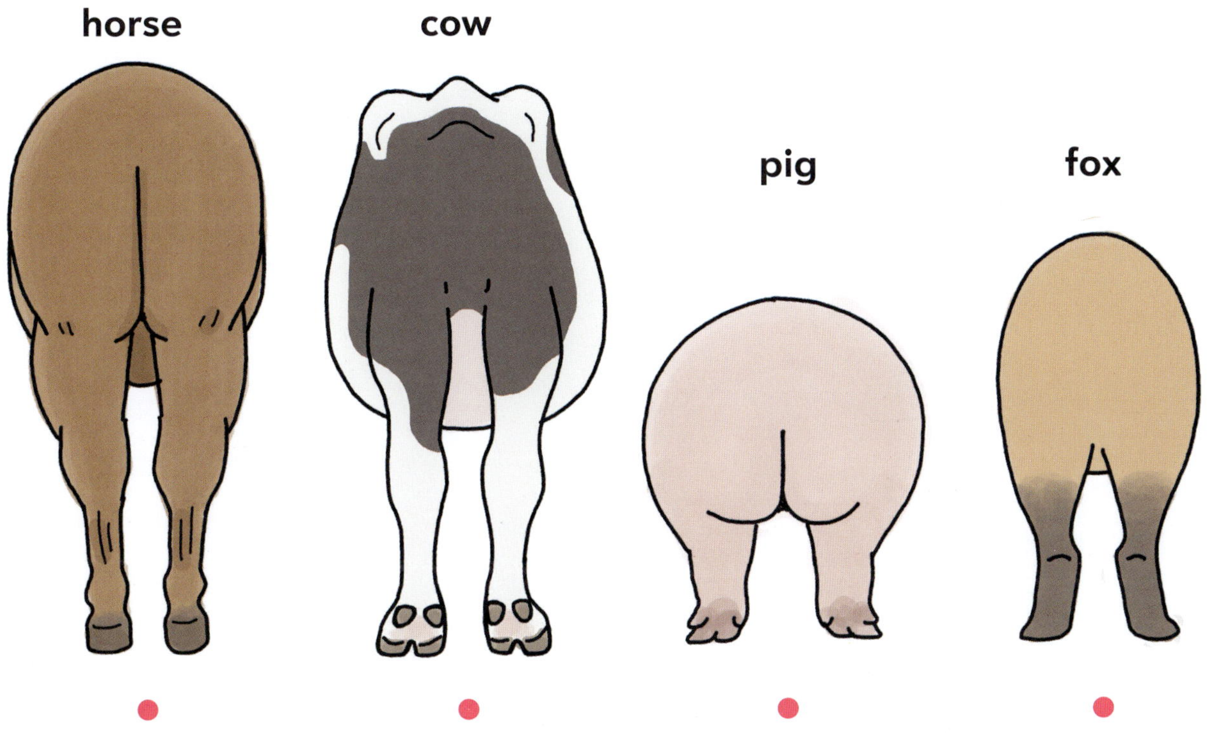

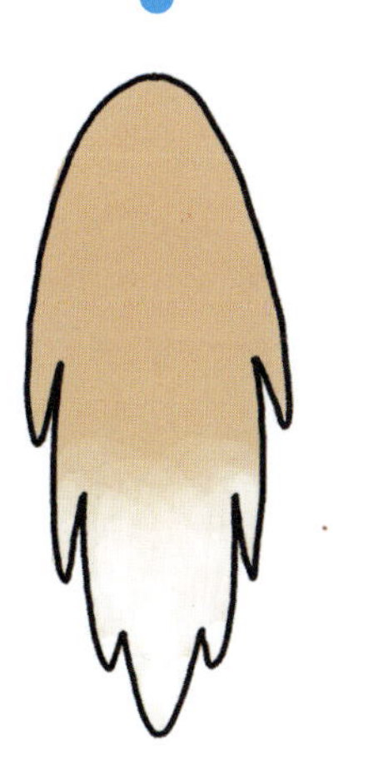

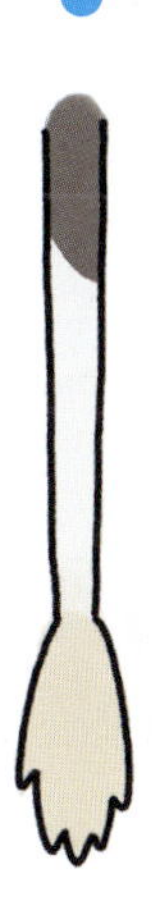

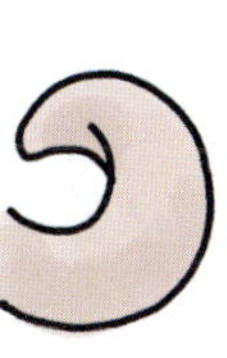

Match the Animal to Its Tail

Draw a line from ● to ● to connect each animal to its tail.

To Parents Squirrels wrap their large tails around their bodies when they sleep to stay warm.

kangaroo

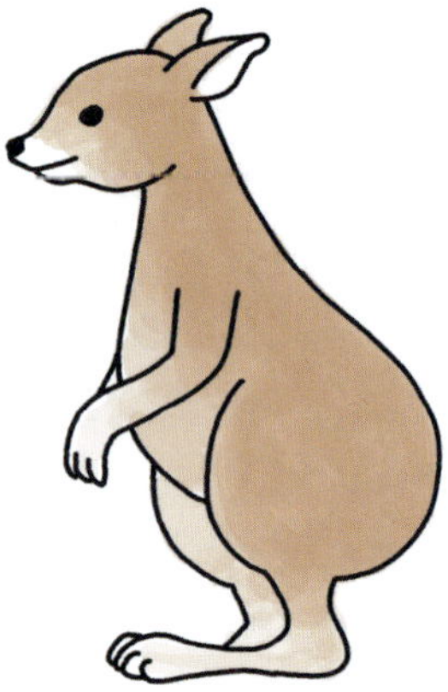

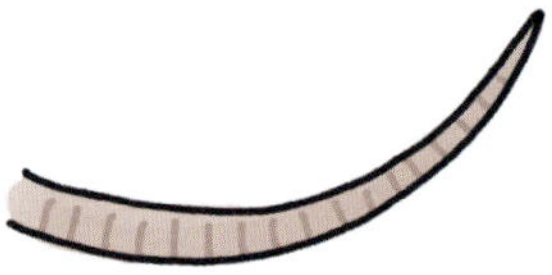

squirrel

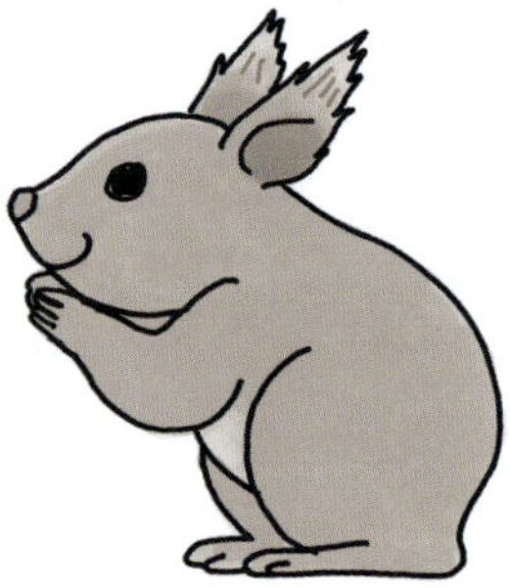

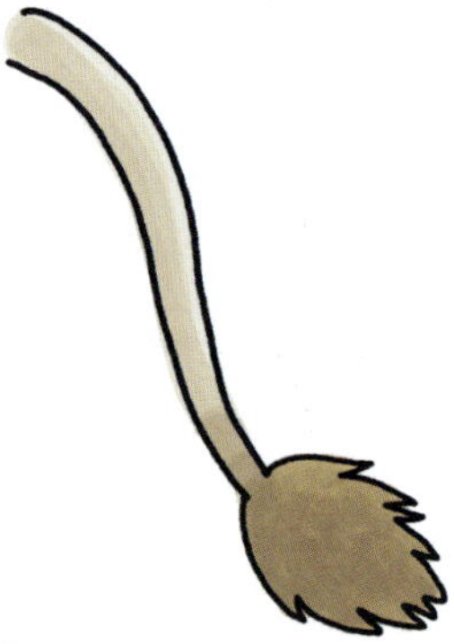

mouse

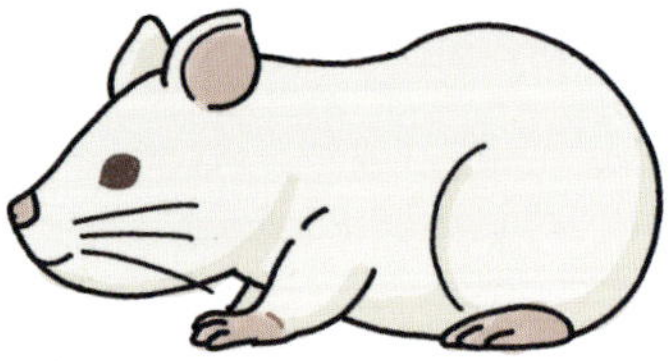

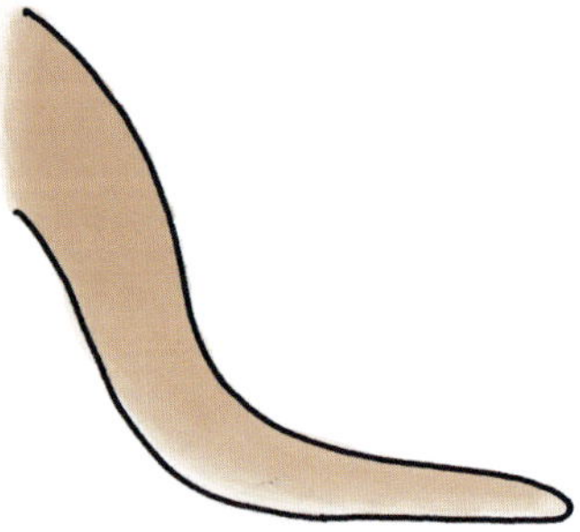

lion

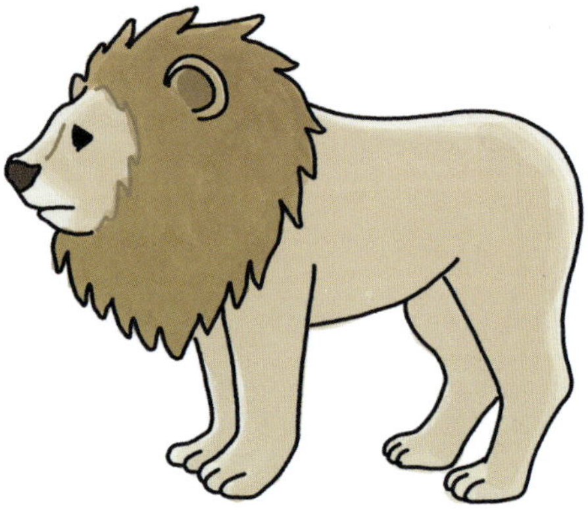

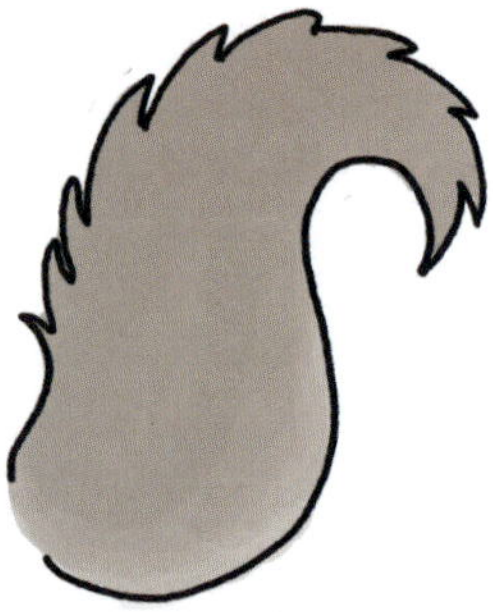

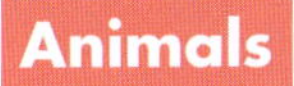

Match the Parent to Its Child

Draw a line from ● to ● to connect each insect to its child.

To Parents Insects that undergo incomplete metamorphosis have three life stages: egg, nymph, and adult. The nymphs look similar to the adults, but they do not have wings.

grasshopper

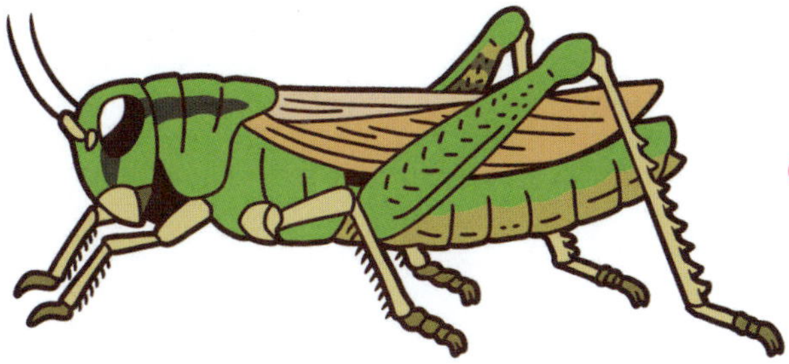

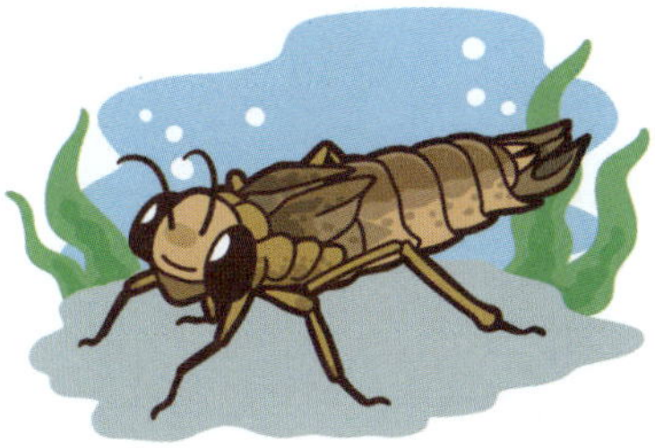

praying mantis

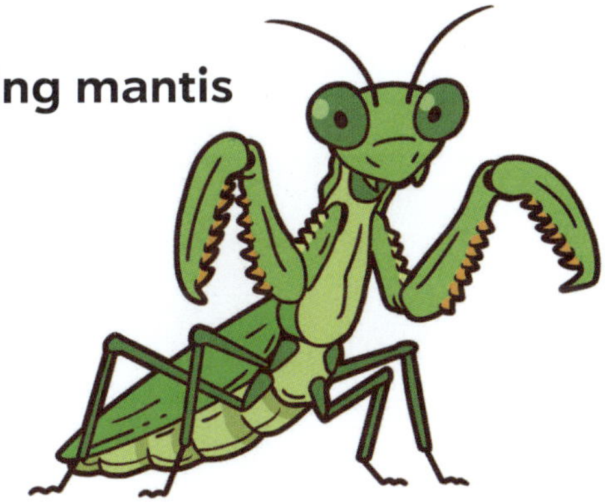

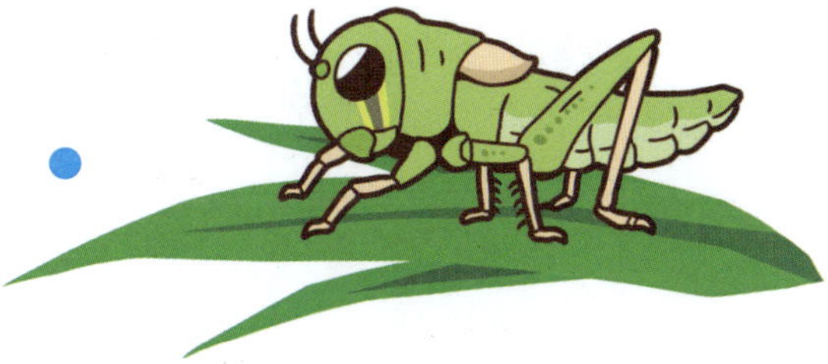

cicada

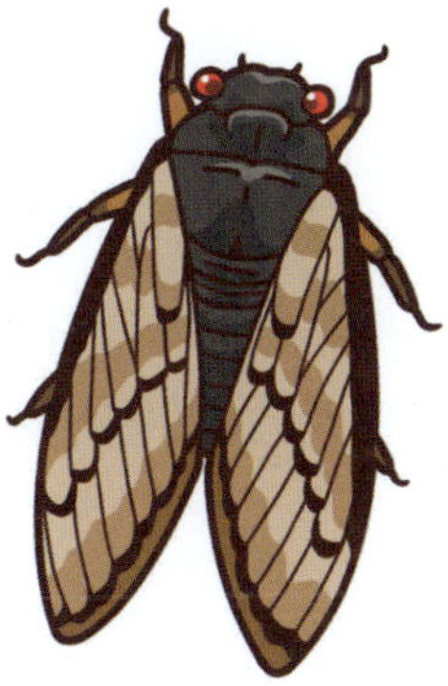

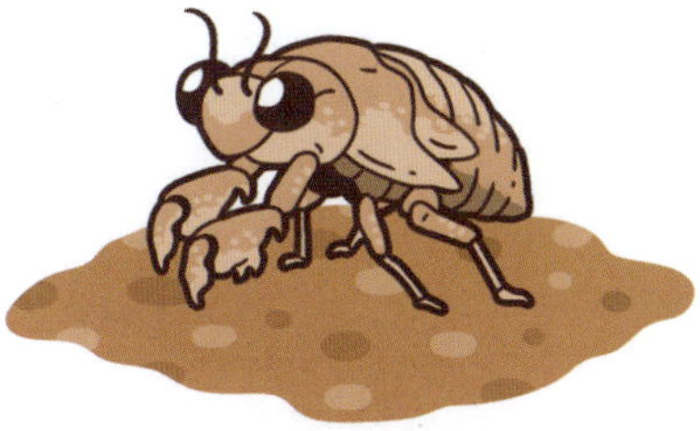

dragonfly

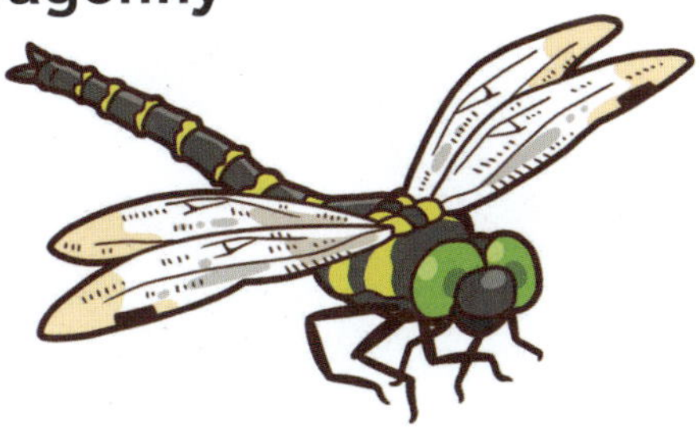

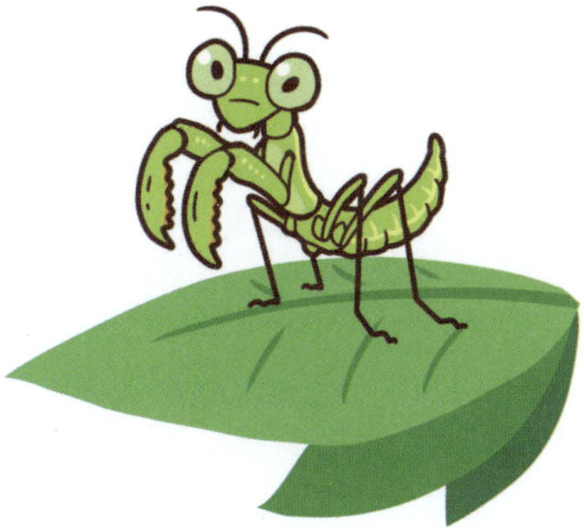

Animals

Match the Parent to Its Child

Draw a line from ● to ● to connect each insect to its larvae.

To Parents The insects on this page undergo complete metamorphosis. They have four life stages: egg, larva, pupa, and adult.

ladybug

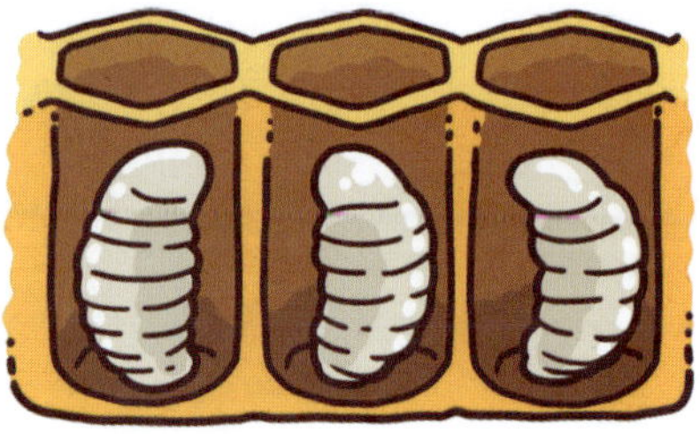

butterfly

ant

bee

Match the Parent to Its Child

Draw a line from ● to ● to connect each animal to its child.

lion

wild boar

deer

malayan tapir

Animals

Match the Parent to Its Child

Draw a line from ● to ● to connect each animal to its child.

To Parents Baby pandas are pink because they have not yet grown all their body hair.

raccoon

bear

panda

hedgehog

Match the Creature to Its Egg

Put the egg stickers next to the matching creatures.

To Parents Animals with backbones are called vertebrates, including fish, amphibians, reptiles, birds, and mammals. While most other animals lay eggs, mammals typically give live birth. However, there are exceptions among fish and reptiles, some of which also give live birth.

frog

sticker

ostrich

sticker

chicken

sticker

sea turtle

sticker

sticker

herring

Write the Numbers in Order

Write the numbers 1 to 4 in the ☐ in the order of growth from egg to butterfly.

To Parents The cabbage butterfly lays its eggs on cruciferous plants such as cabbage. The larvae feed on the leaves of cruciferous plants and grow up, undergoing a transformation inside a chrysalis to become adults.

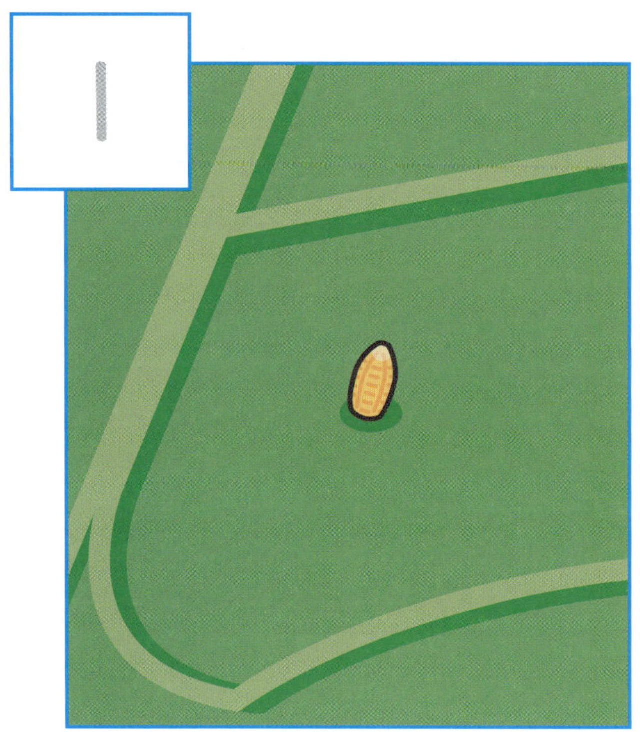

Match the Insect to Its Food

Draw a line from ● to ● to connect each insect to its food.

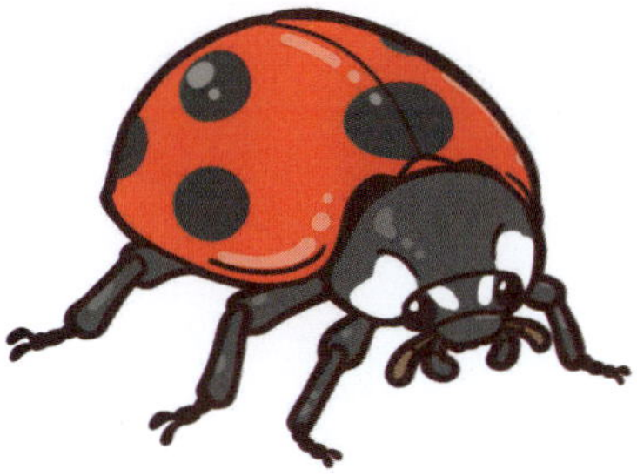

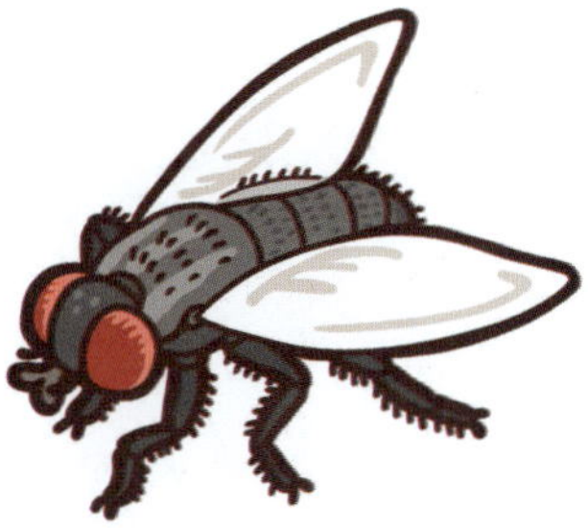

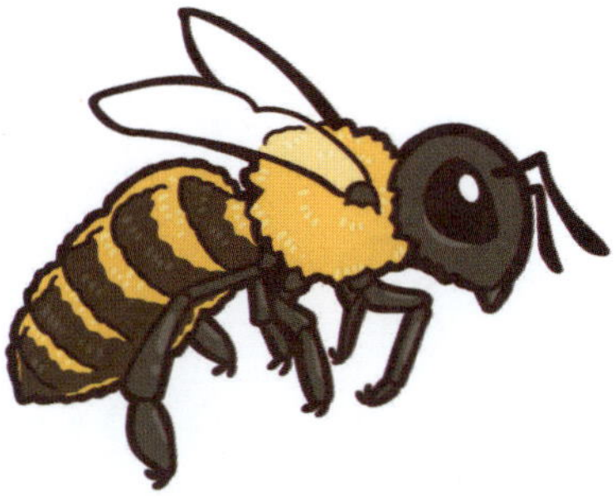

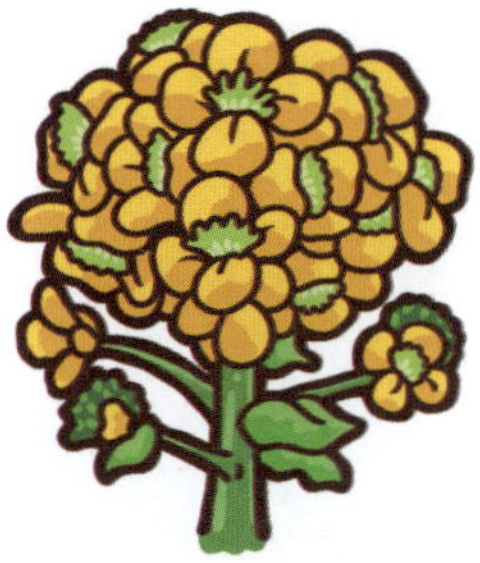

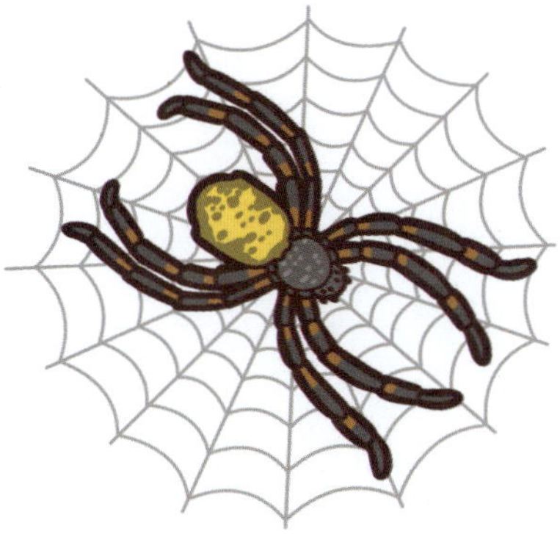

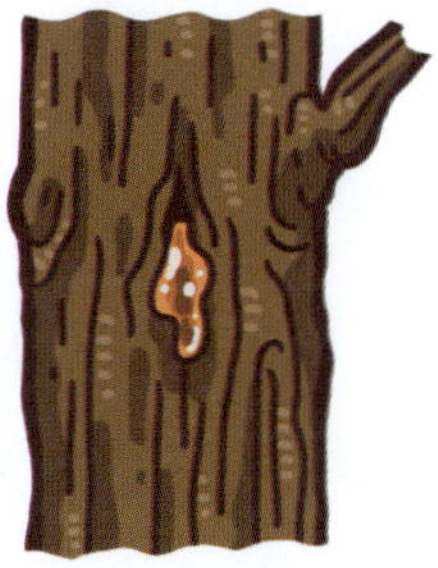

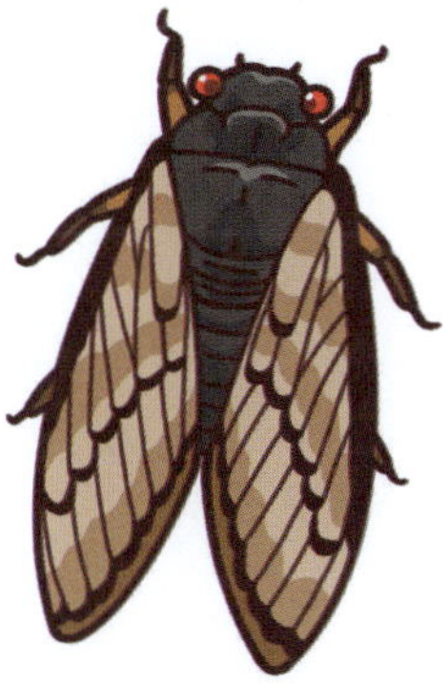

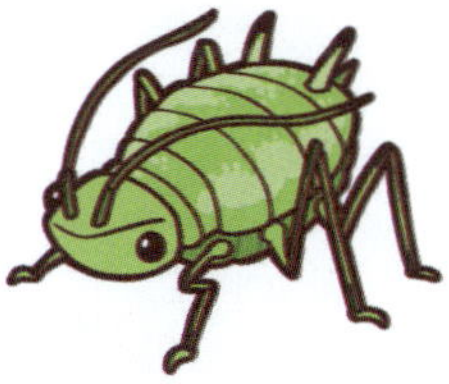

Match the Animal to Its Food

Draw a line from ● to ● to connect each animal to its food.

Animals

Find Extinct Creatures

Find five extinct creatures and draw a ○ in the (　) near them.

To Parents Dinosaurs thrived on Earth for about 160 million years and became extinct about 66 million years ago. The saber-toothed tiger, on the other hand, became extinct about 10,000 years ago.

diplodocus (　　)

lizard (　　)

triceratops (　　)

rhinoceros (　　)

tyrannosaurus (　　)

stegosaurus (　　)

bat (　　)

saber-toothed tiger (　　)

Earth Science

How the Wind Blows

Put the handkerchief and T-shirt stickers on the clothesline so they can blow in the wind.

To Parents Air movement creates wind. The laundry catches the wind and flutters from windward to leeward.

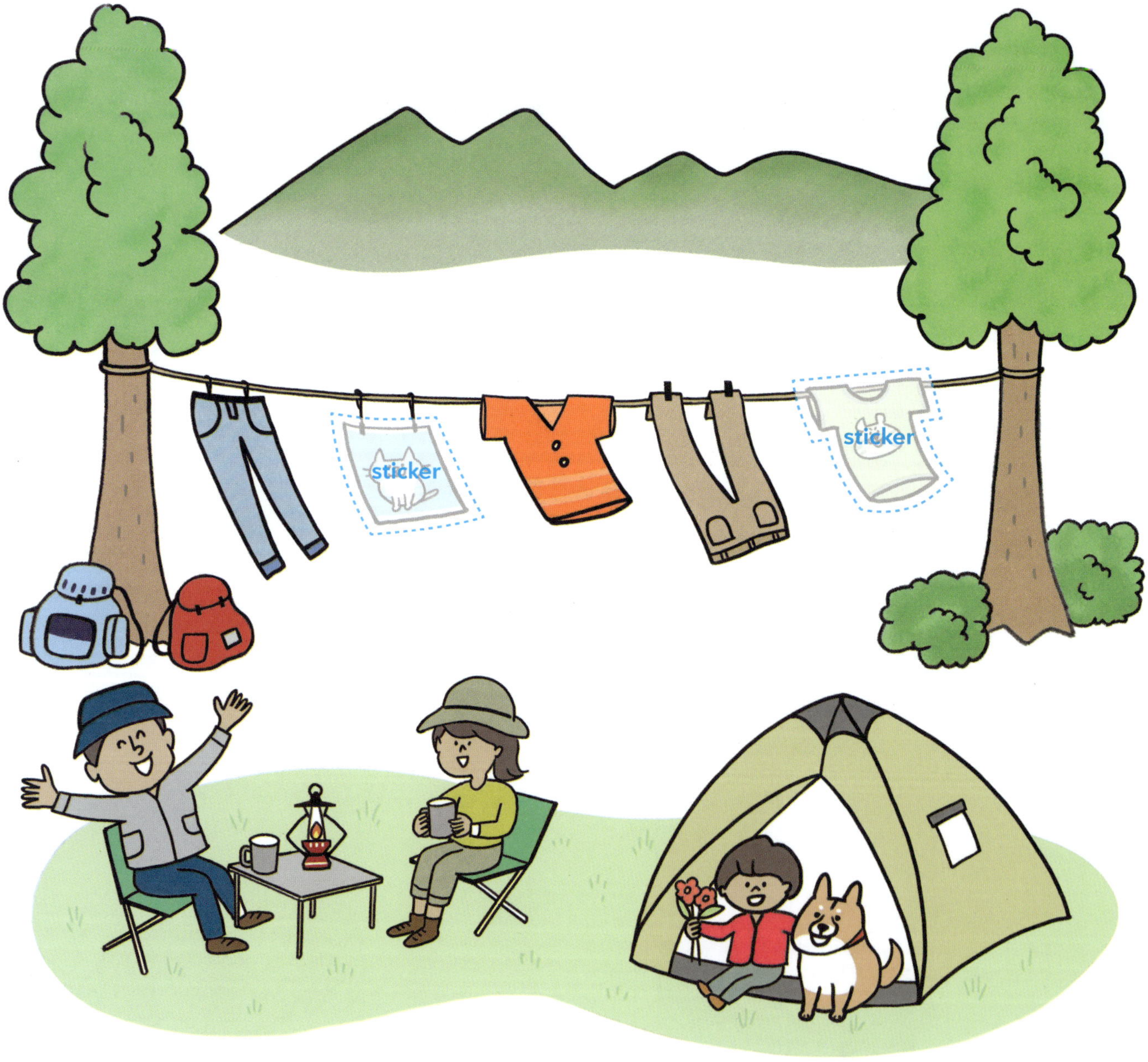

Earth Science

How the Wind Blows

Find three mistakes in the picture by paying attention to the wind direction, and draw an X on each of them.

To Parents Air is invisible, but it has power. Air moving from right to left moves anything it hits from right to left.

Direction of the wind

Earth Science

Find the Strongest Wind

Find the picture showing the strongest wind, and draw a ○ in the (   ) below it.

(   )   (   )   (   )

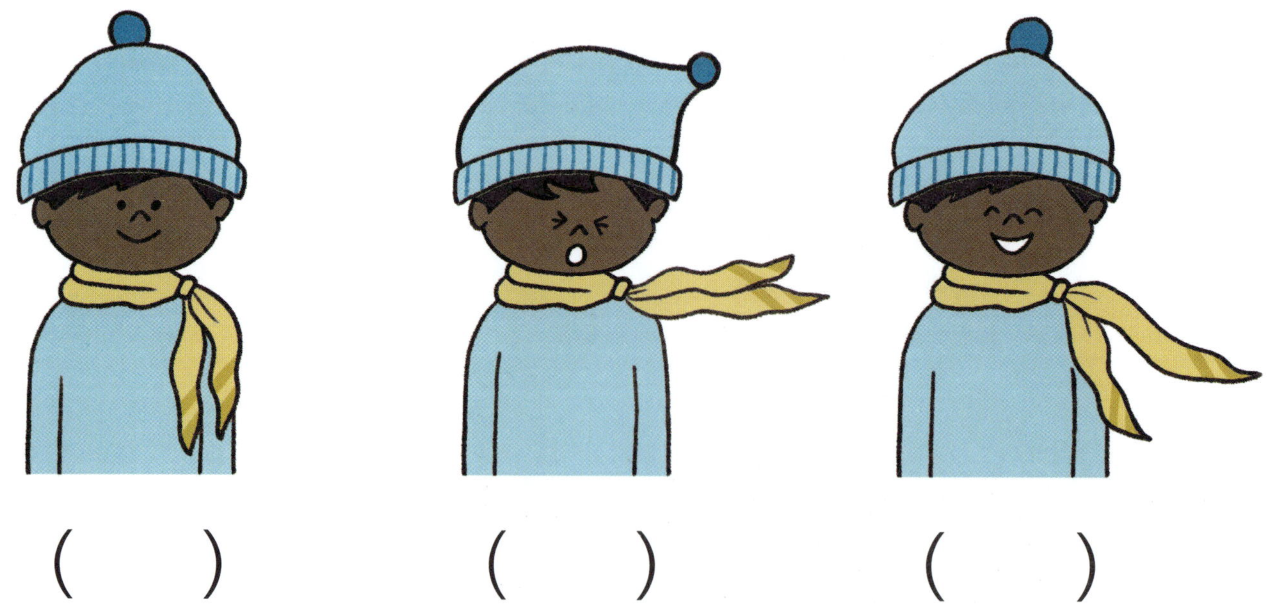

(   )   (   )   (   )

Earth Science

Write the Numbers in Order

Write the numbers 1 to 4 in the □ in order from lightest wind to strongest wind.

To Parents Pay attention to the angle of the umbrella and the position of the hands supporting it.

Earth Science

Which Is the Correct Shadow?

Find the correct shadow of the tree by paying attention to the position of the sun, and draw a ○ in the ( ) next to it.

To Parents Shadows are the areas of darkness created when an object blocks the light.

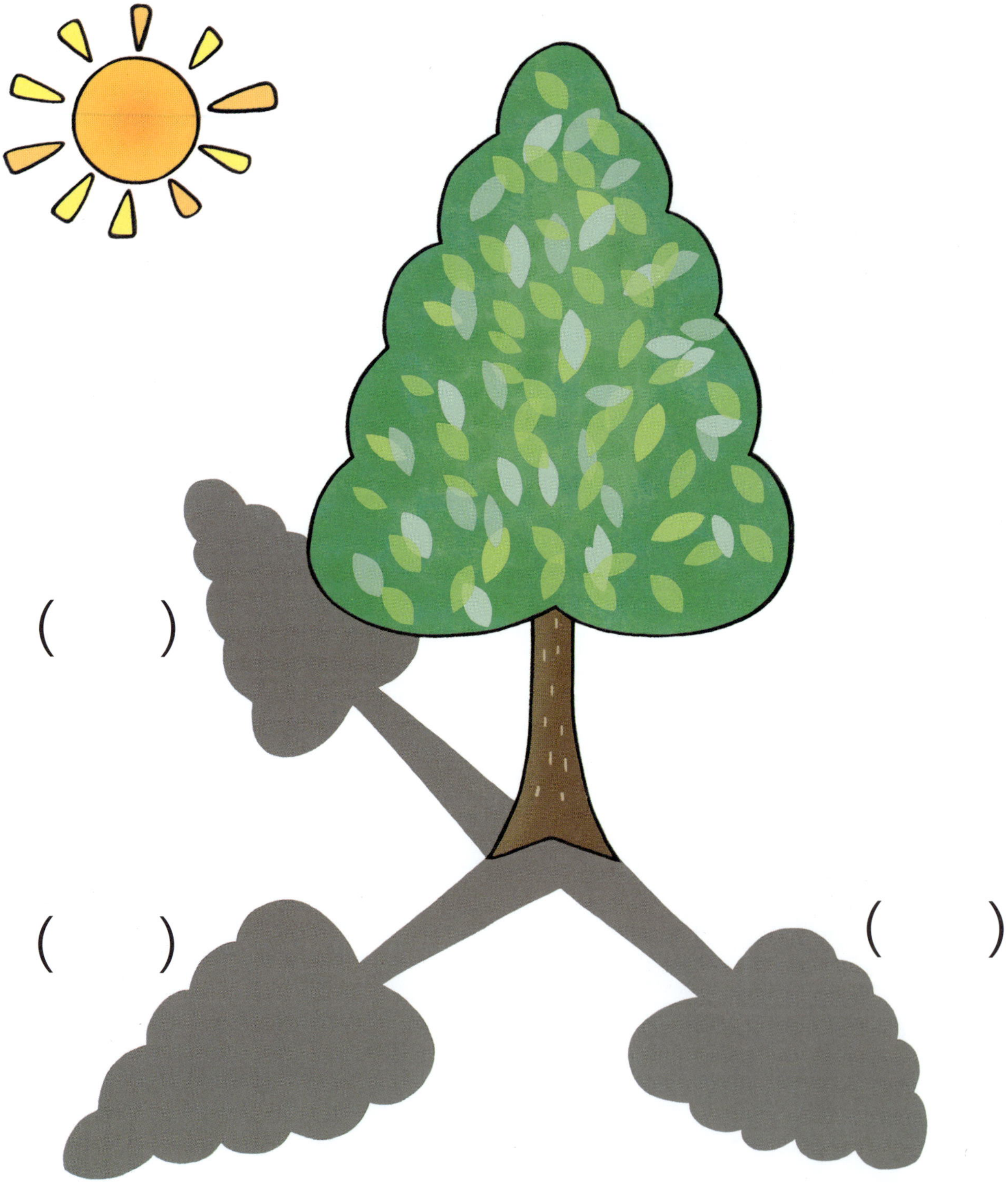

( )

( )

( )

Earth Science

How the Sun Creates Shadows

Find the incorrect shadows by paying attention to the position of the sun and the shape of the shadows, and draw an X in the ( ) near them.

To Parents Some of the shadows on this page are drawn somewhat incorrectly. Look carefully at the direction and shape of the shadows in reference to the sun.

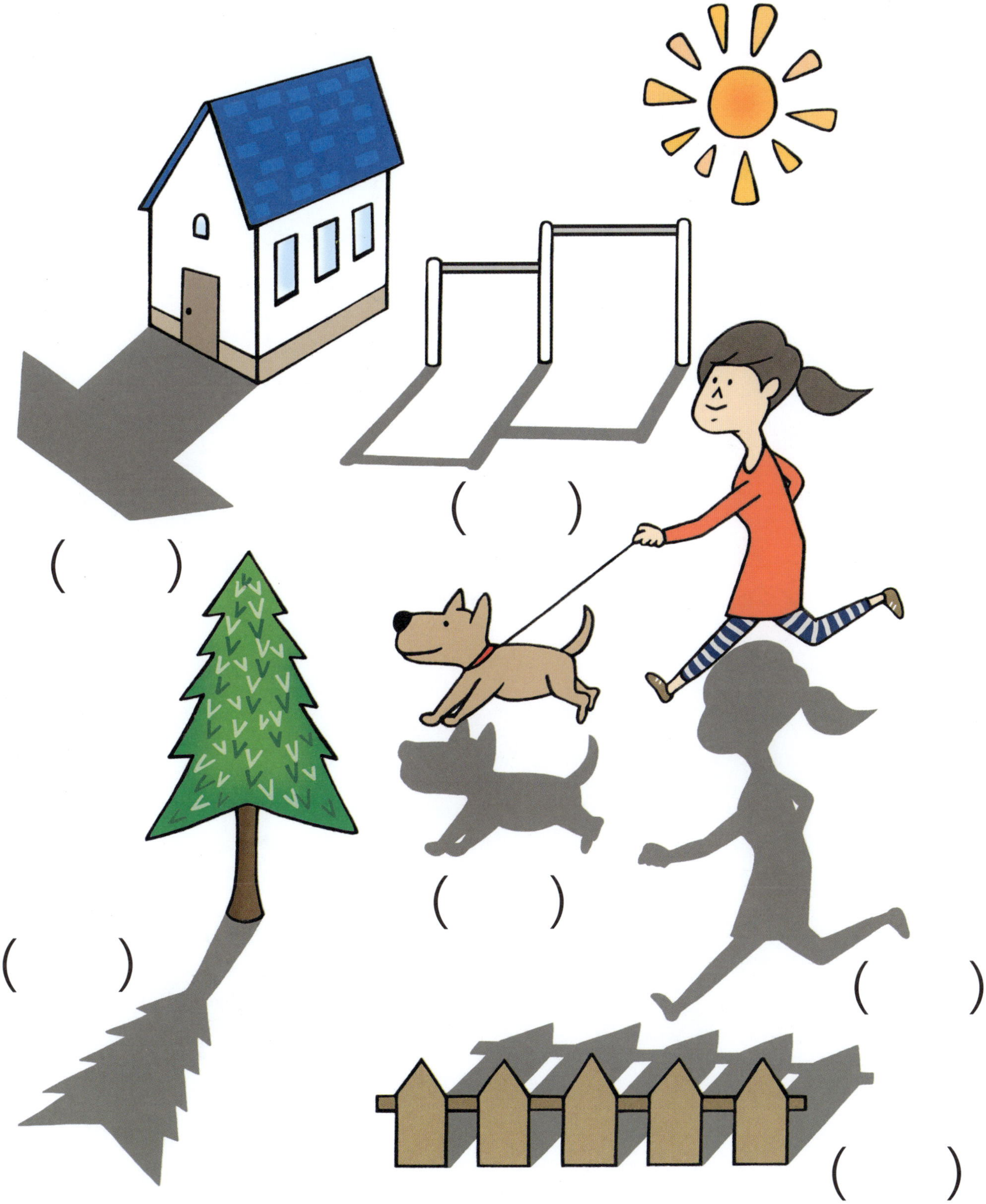

( ) ( ) ( ) ( ) ( ) ( )

Earth Science

Place the Shadow Stickers

GOOD JOB!

Put a shadow sticker on each matching shape.

Earth Science

How the Sun Creates Shadows

Find the image where the order of the shadows matches the movement of the sun from ① to ③, and draw a ◯ in the (　) next to it.

To Parents From morning to evening, shadows are constantly moving. The shadows created by the sun move in the opposite direction from the sun.

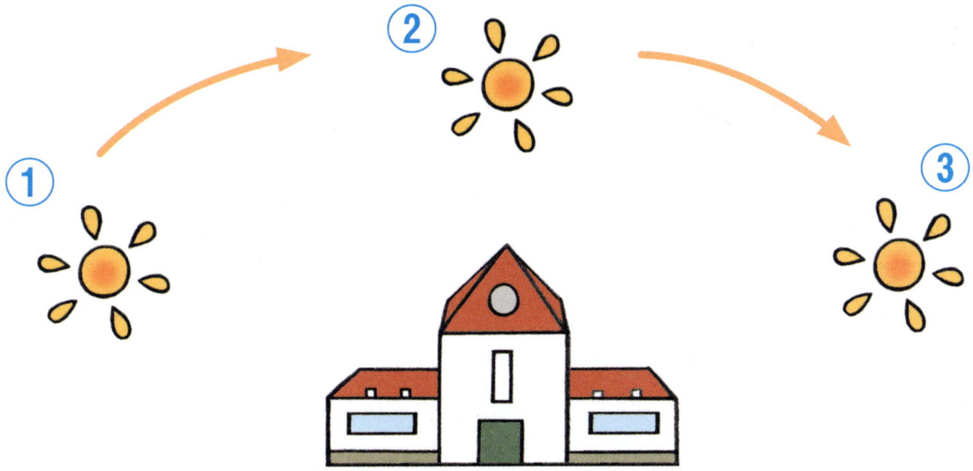

①　②　③

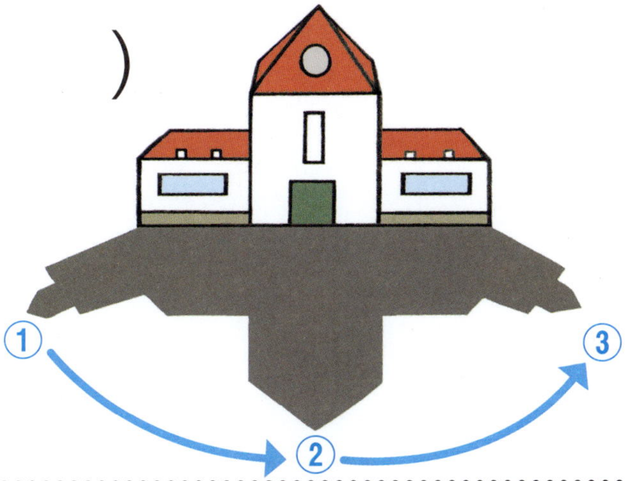

(　　)　① ② ③

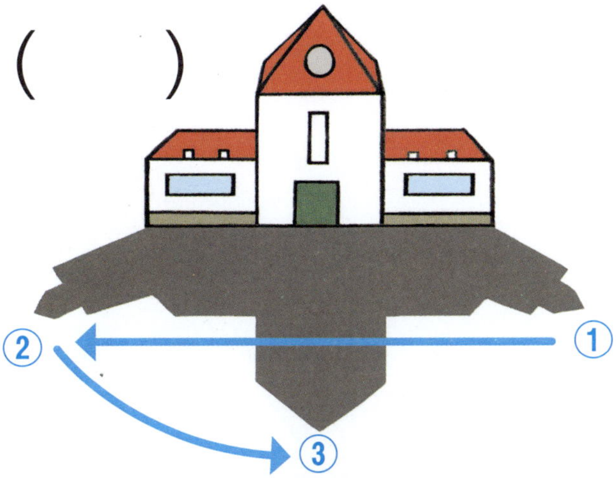

(　　)　② ① ③

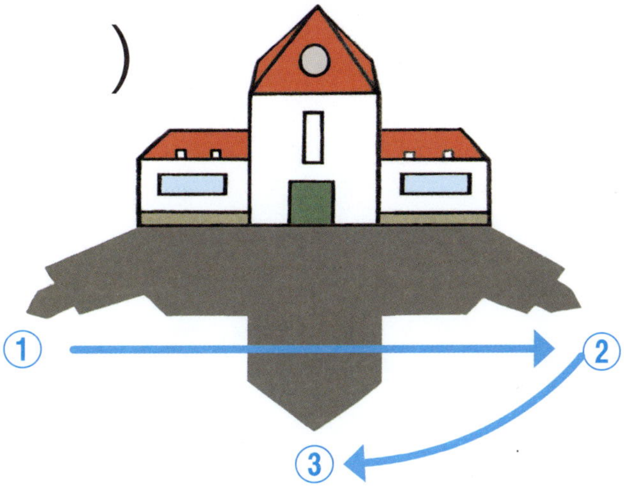

(　　)　① ② ③

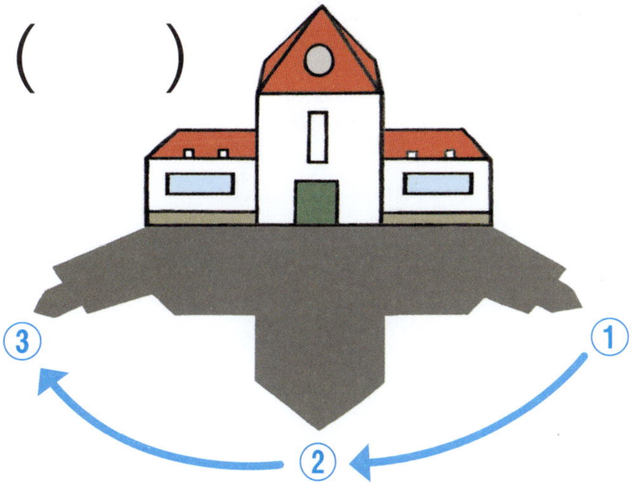

(　　)　③ ① ②

Physical Science

Find the Correct Shadow

Find what happens to the shadows of the red and blue cards when they are stacked on top of each other, and draw a ◯ in the (   ) below it.

To Parents Shadows of opaque objects are black. The color of the shadow does not change when opaque objects are stacked.

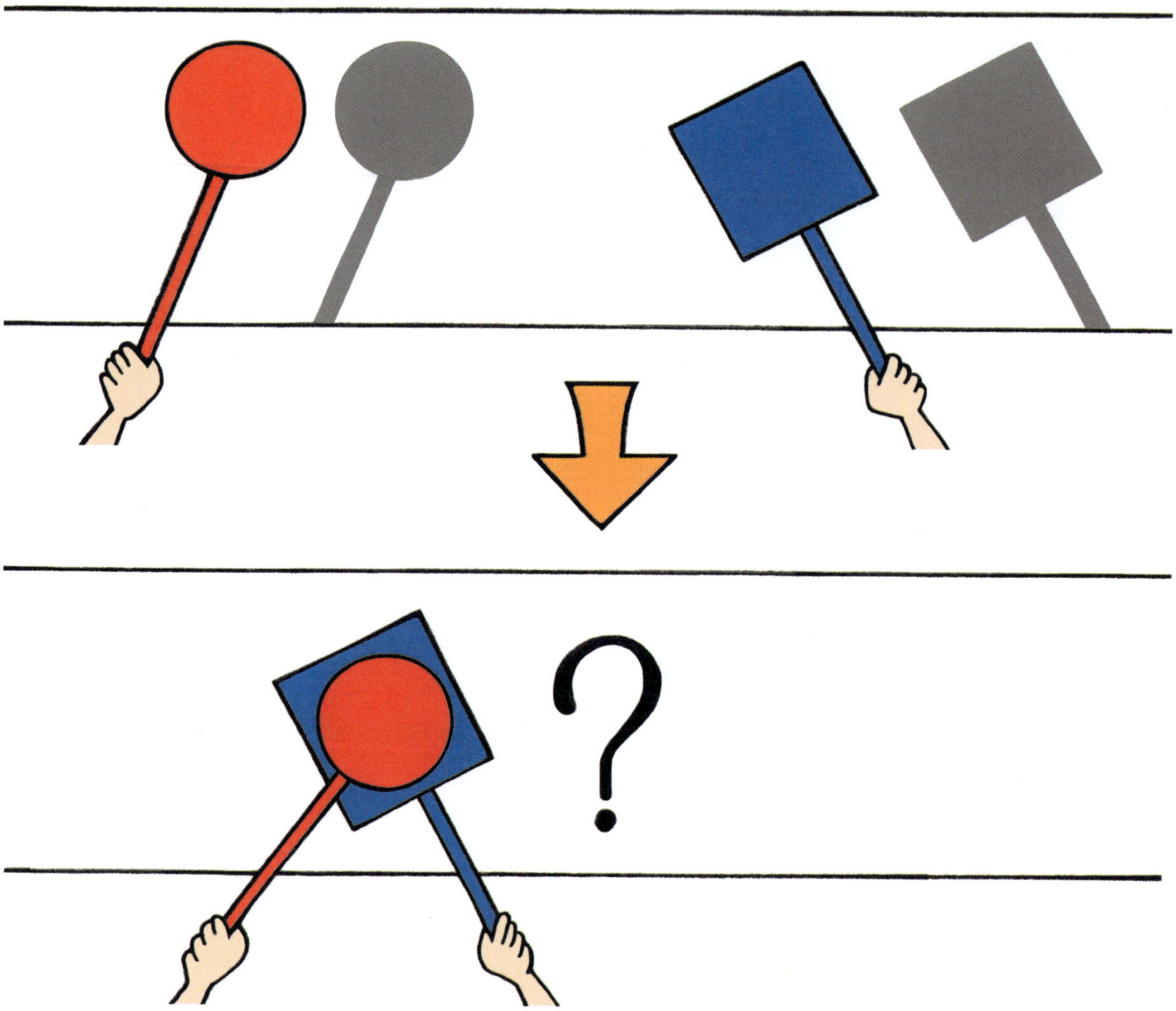

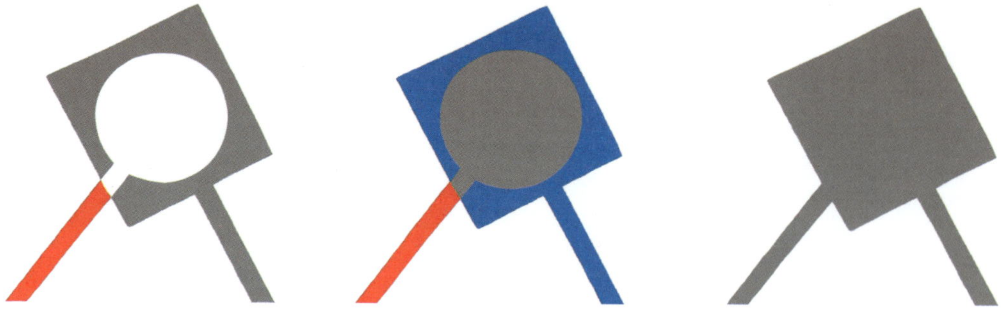

?

(   ) (   ) (   )

Physical Science

Find the Correct Shadow

Find the correct shadow, and draw a ◯ in the (   ) next to it.

To Parents The shape of a shadow changes depending on the way the light hits an object. Observe the shadows of opaque, transparent, and colored translucent objects.

(   )

(   )

(   )

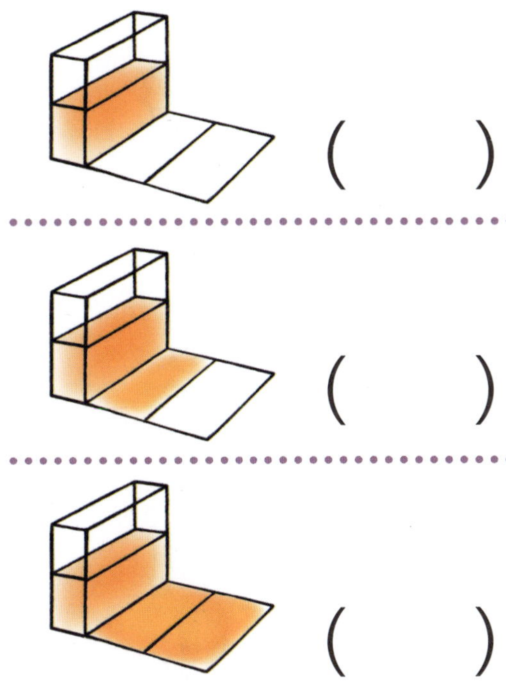

(   )

(   )

(   )

Physical Science

Find the Correct Shadow

Draw a line from ● to ● to connect each doll to its shadow.

GOOD JOB!

To Parents If you hold the flashlight close to the doll, the shadow will be large and have blurred edges. As you move the flashlight farther away from the doll, the shadow will become smaller, with more defined edges.

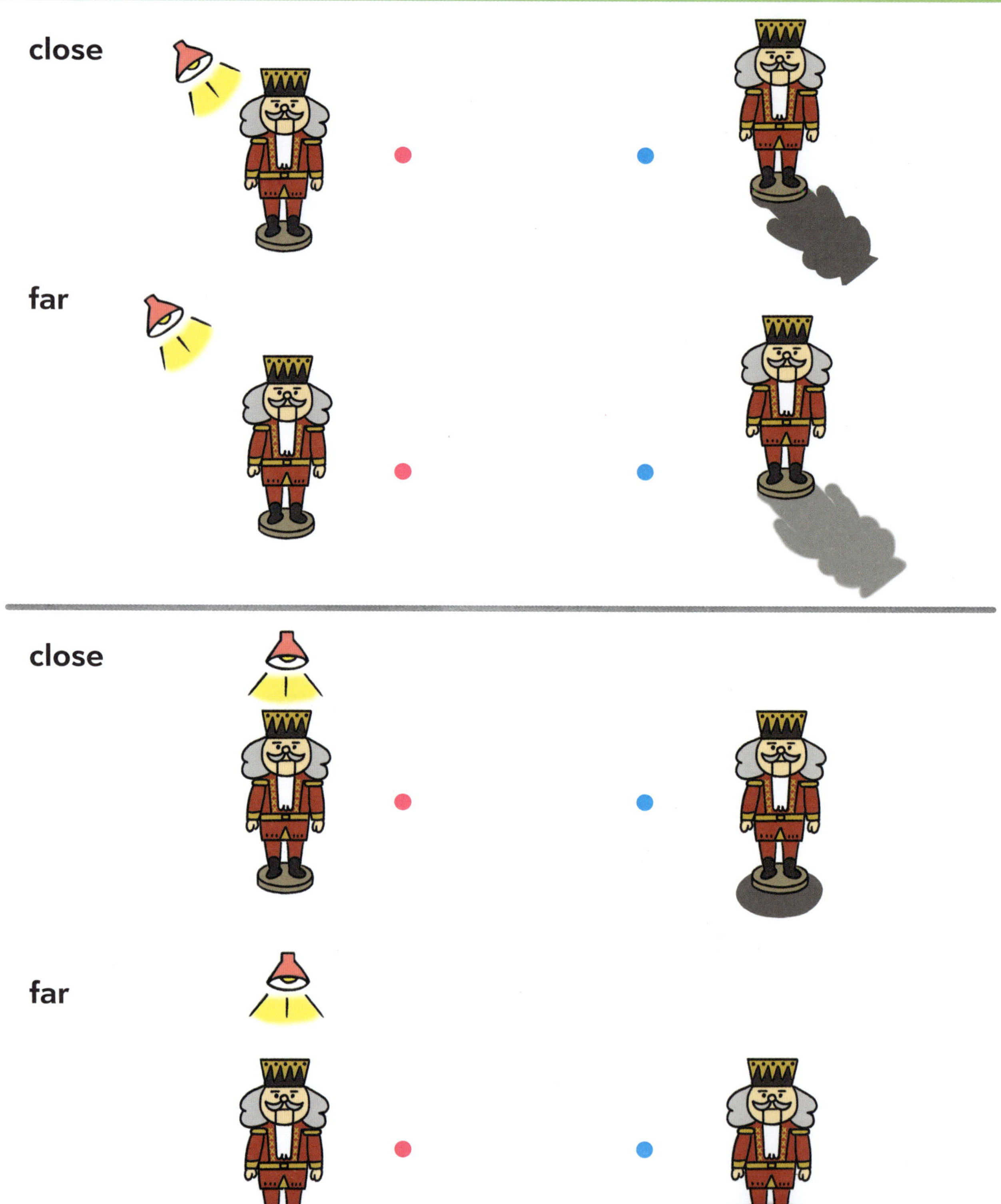

Physical Science

Find the Correct Shadow

What shadows will be cast on the man's face when light is shone on it from positions 1 to 4? Write the number of the position below each face.

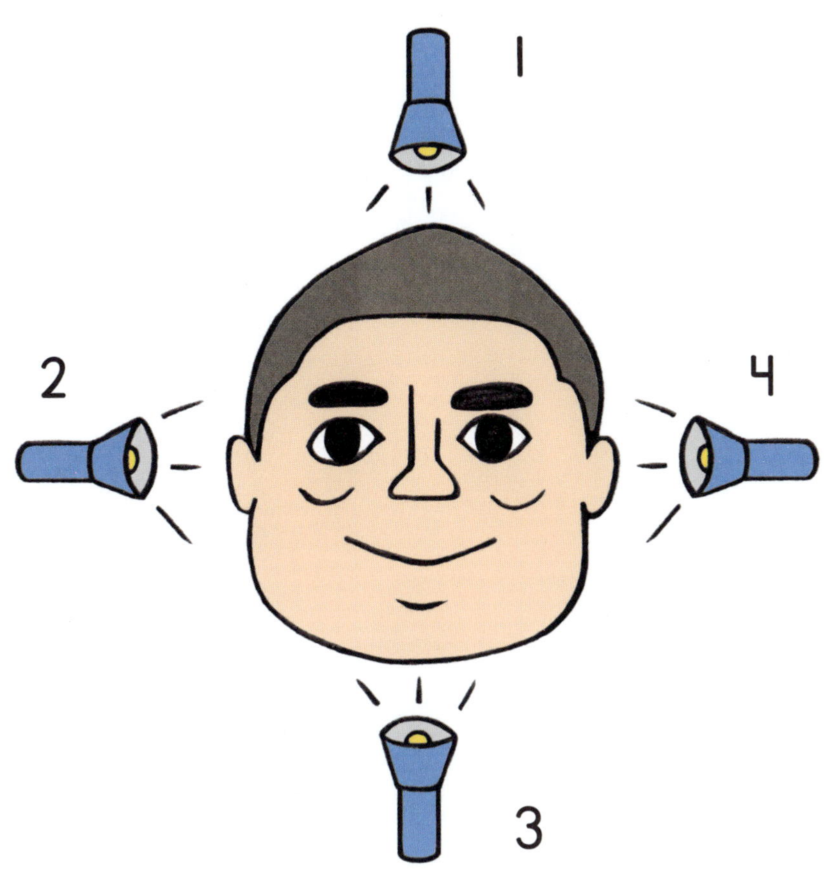

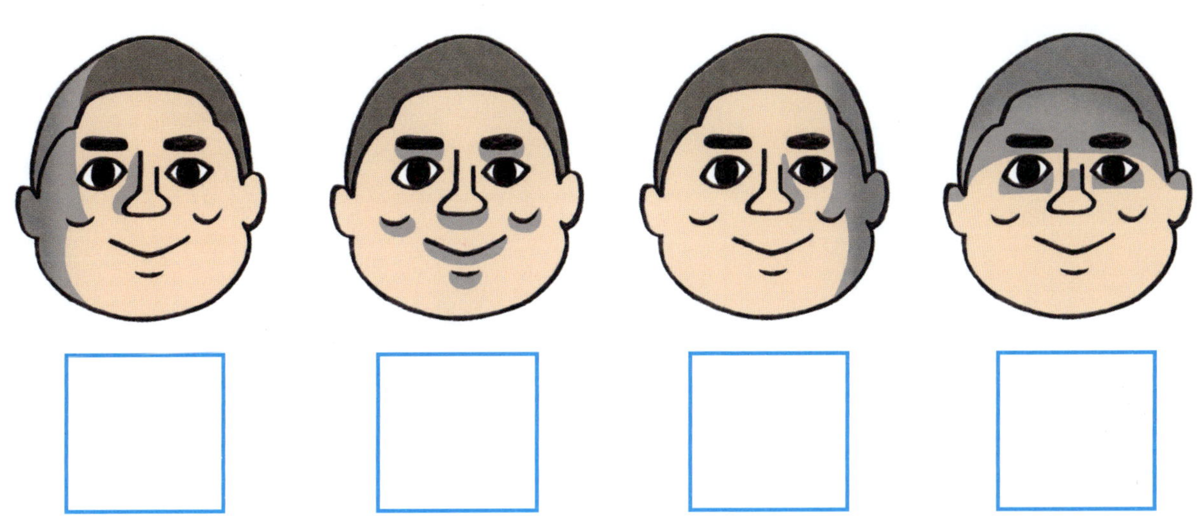

Earth Science

Write the Numbers in Order

Write the numbers 1 to 4 in the ☐ in the order in which the snowman changes.

To Parents Sunlight has heat. The snowman melts in the sunlight.

Earth Science

Write the Numbers in Order

Write the numbers 1 to 3 in the □ in the order in which the snowmen will melt, from fastest to slowest.

To Parents Snow melts differently in the sun and in the shade because of the difference in temperature. Snow that is in the shade all day melts very slowly.

Earth Science

Find the Color of the Rainbow

Find the rainbow with the correct color sequence, and draw a ◯ in the ( ) below it.

To Parents Sunlight is a mixture of many colors. When it passes through drops of water, the colors appear to separate, forming a rainbow. Red has the longest wavelength so it appears on the outside of the rainbow.

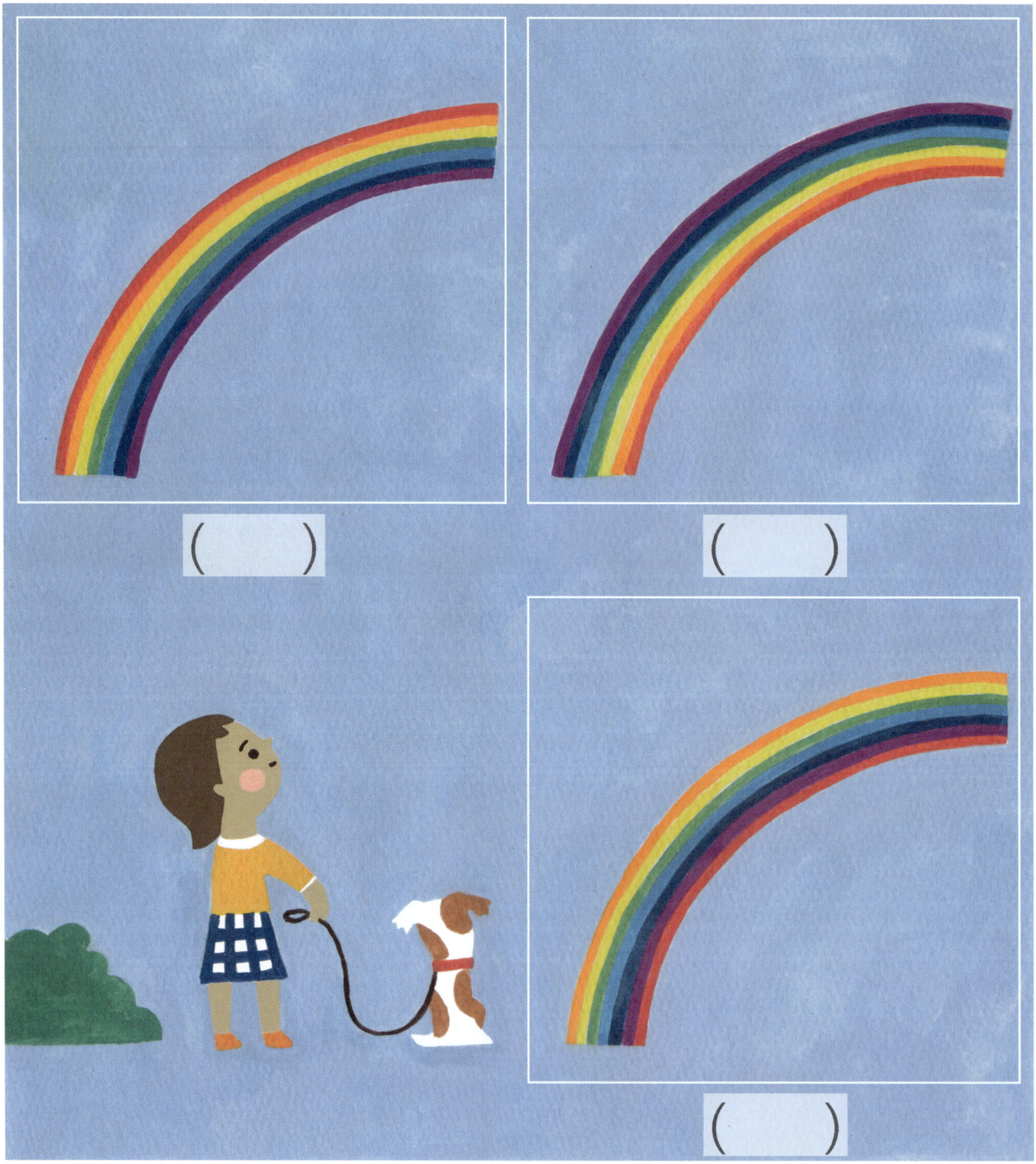

( )

( )

( )

Physical Science

Which Machines Must Be Plugged In?

Find the machines that require an electrical outlet, and draw a ○ in the ( ) below them.

To Parents Some household appliances are powered by electricity that they get from electrical outlets. To work, they must be plugged in.

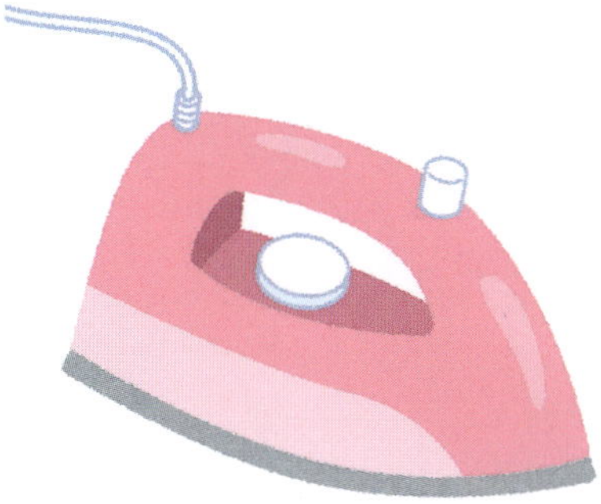

iron (   )

kettle (   )

wind-up toy (   )

music box (   )

TV (   )

wood stove (   )

lantern (   )

Physical Science

Which Vehicles Are Human-Powered?

Find the vehicles that move solely by human power, and draw a ○ in the (   ) below them.

To Parents Cars and motorcycles run on gasoline, diesel fuel, or electricity.

car (   )

rowboat (   )

bicycle (   )

skateboard (   )

tricycle (   )

motorcycle (   )

Physical Science

Write the Numbers in Order

Write the numbers 1 to 4 in the (　) in order of size, from the biggest to the smallest.

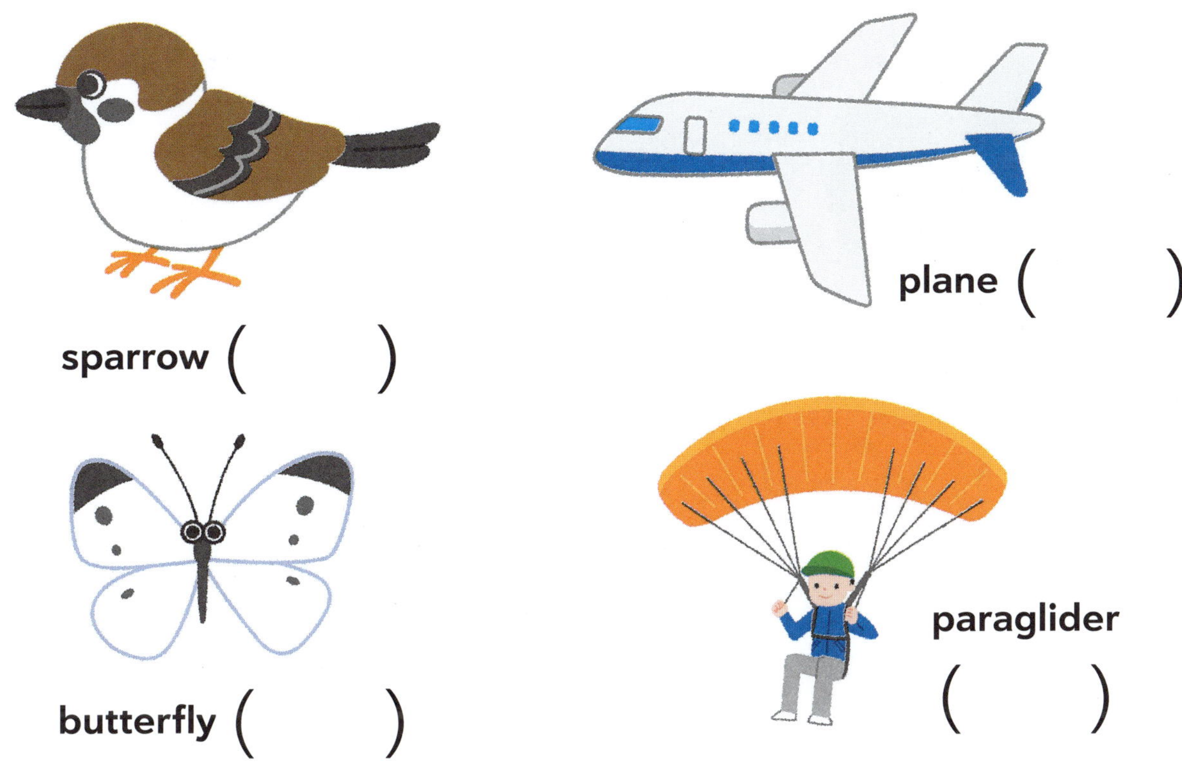

Physical Science

Write the Numbers in Order

Write the numbers 1 to 4 in the (   ) in order of size, from the smallest to the biggest.

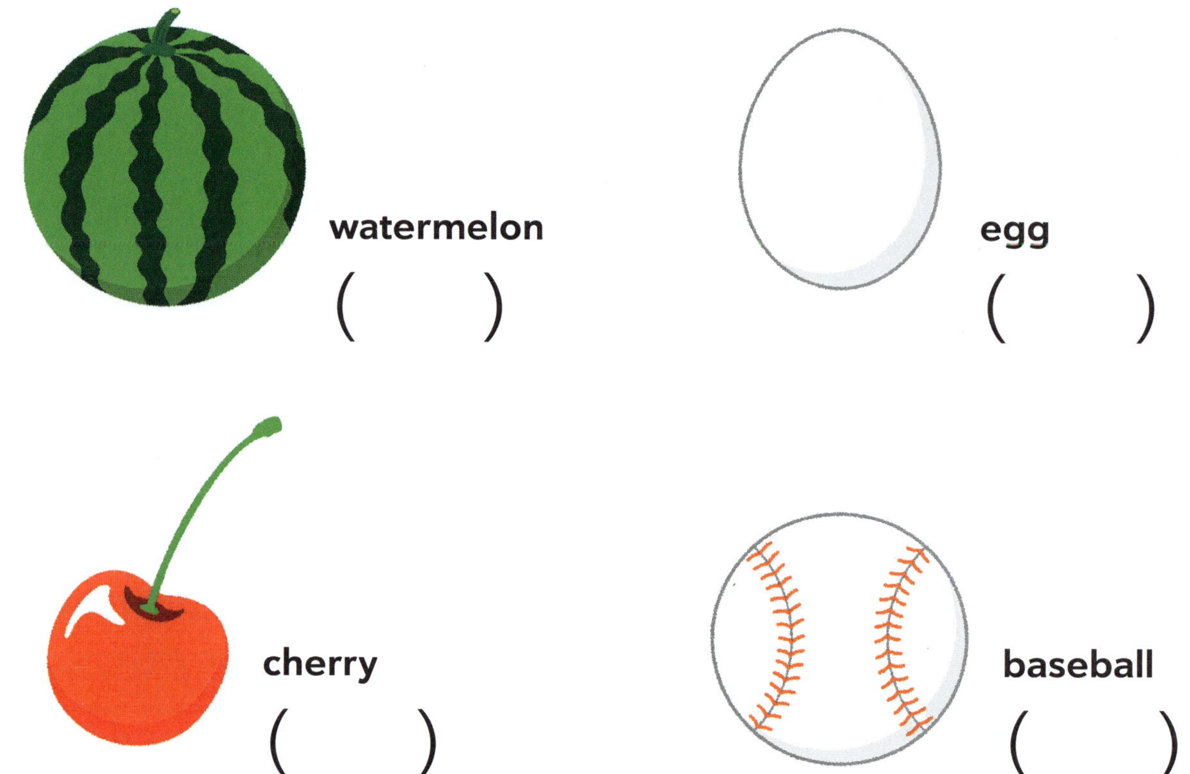

Physical Science

Write the Numbers in Order

Write the numbers 1 to 3 in the (   ) in order from sweetest to least sweet.

To Parents When the amount of tea stays the same and the amount of sugar is doubled, the tea becomes sweeter. When the amount of tea is doubled but the amount of sugar stays the same, the tea becomes less sweet.

(   )

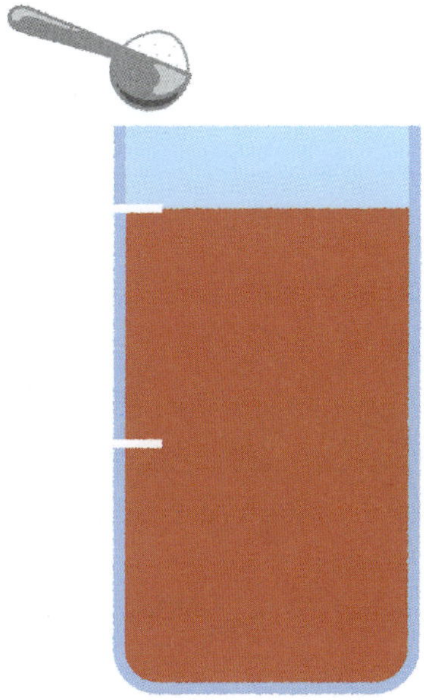

(   )

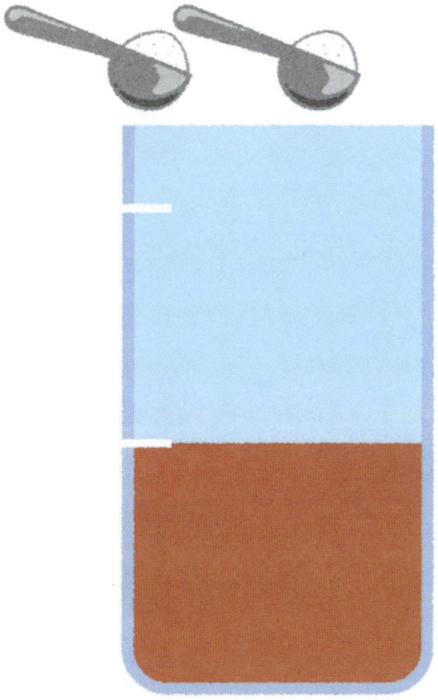

(   )

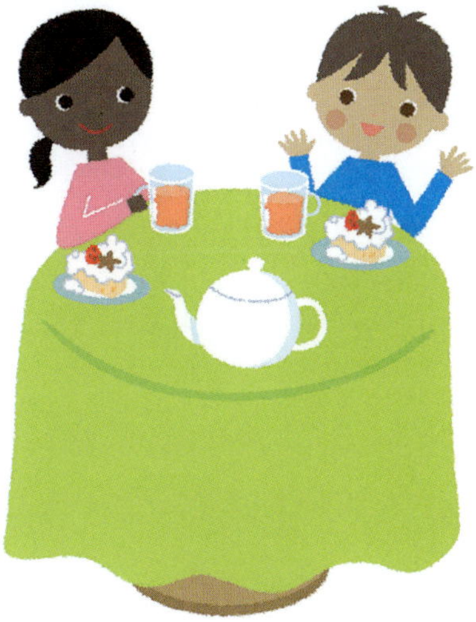

Physical Science

Place the Tea Color Stickers

Put a sticker on each teacup to show the color of the tea after lemon or honey has been added.

To Parents Black tea becomes lighter in color when it reacts with the acidity of lemon juice. The tannins in black tea can react with iron ions. If the honey contains sufficient trace iron, this reaction will occur upon addition, causing the tea to become darker.

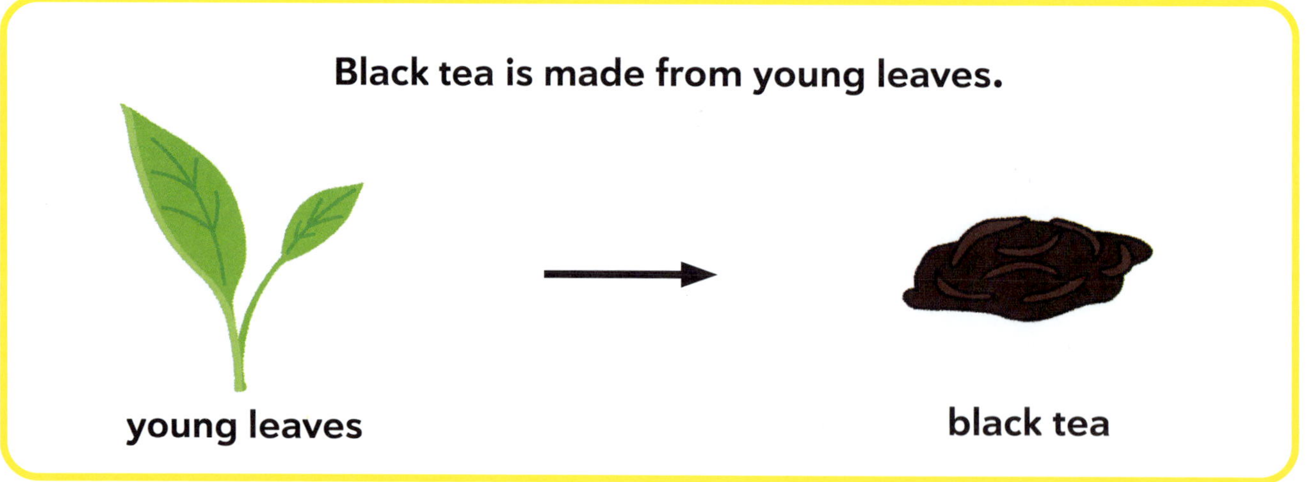

Physical Science

Write the Numbers in Order

Write the numbers 1 to 4 in the ☐ in order from the highest bounce to the lowest when the girl drops the ball.

To Parents A ball's momentum increases as it falls. So the higher the drop, the higher the bounce, if the floor is the same.

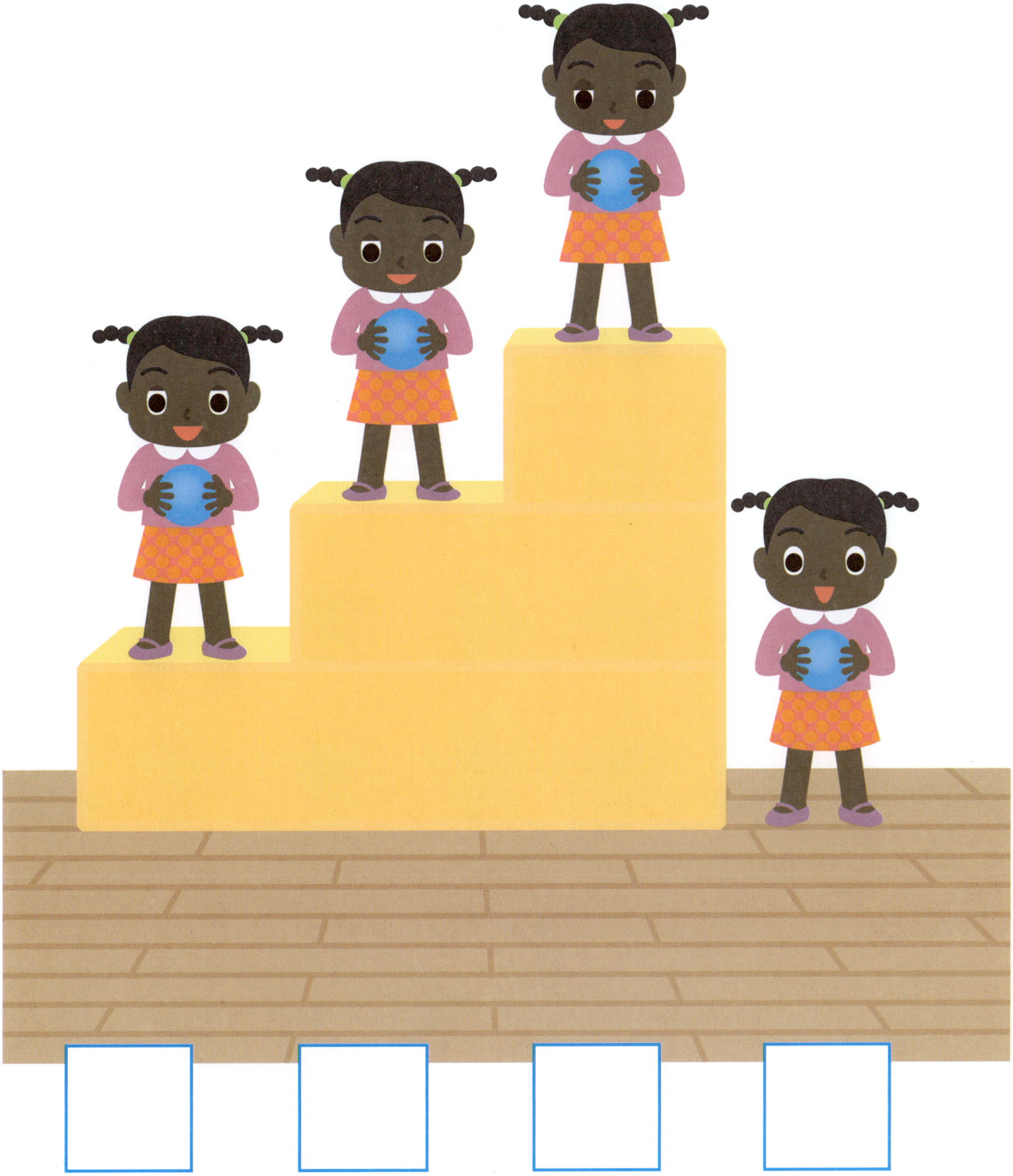

☐ ☐ ☐ ☐

Physical Science

Write the Numbers in Order

Write the numbers 1 to 4 in the ☐ in order from the highest bounce to the lowest when the boy drops the ball. Pay attention to the type of ground.

To Parents When balls are dropped from the same height, the ones that hit a hard surface bounce higher. This is because soft surfaces absorb more of the force of the fall than hard surfaces.

grass

concrete

grass

☐ ☐ ☐ ☐

Physical Science

How Mirrors Reflect

Find the correct reflection in the mirror, and draw a ◯ in the ( ) next to it.

( )

( )

( )

( )

( )

( )

Physical Science

How the Pond Reflects

Find the correct reflections on the surface of the pond, and draw a ○ in the (   ) below them.

To Parents The pond is like a mirror lying on the ground. If your child has difficulty understanding, turn the book on its side.

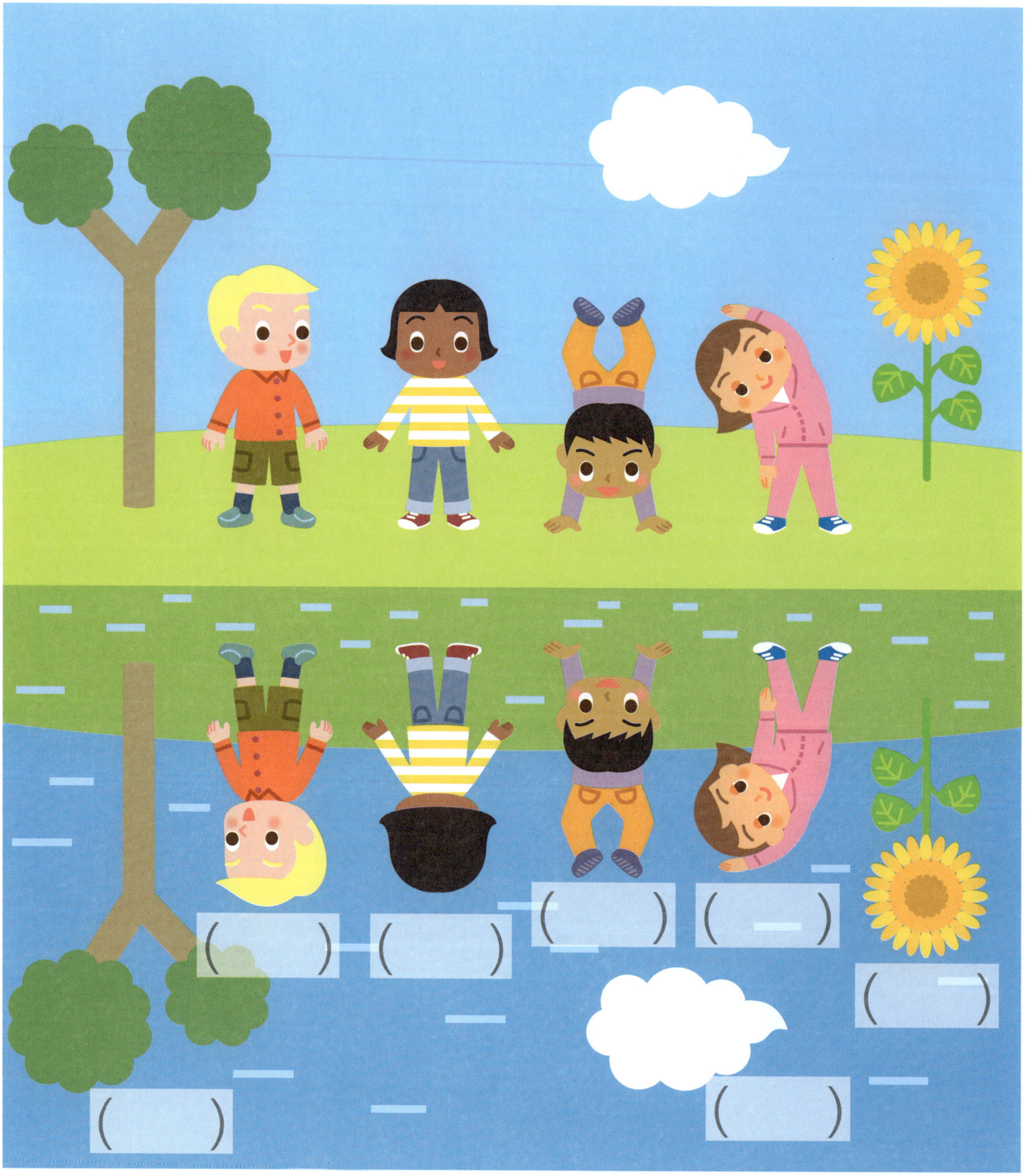

(   ) (   ) (   ) (   ) (   ) (   ) (   )

Physical Science

How the Water Changes

Find the picture that shows what happens when the rock is placed in the glass of water, and draw a ◯ in the (   ) below it.

To Parents When solids that do not dissolve in water are added to water, the water is displaced by their volume, and the water level rises.

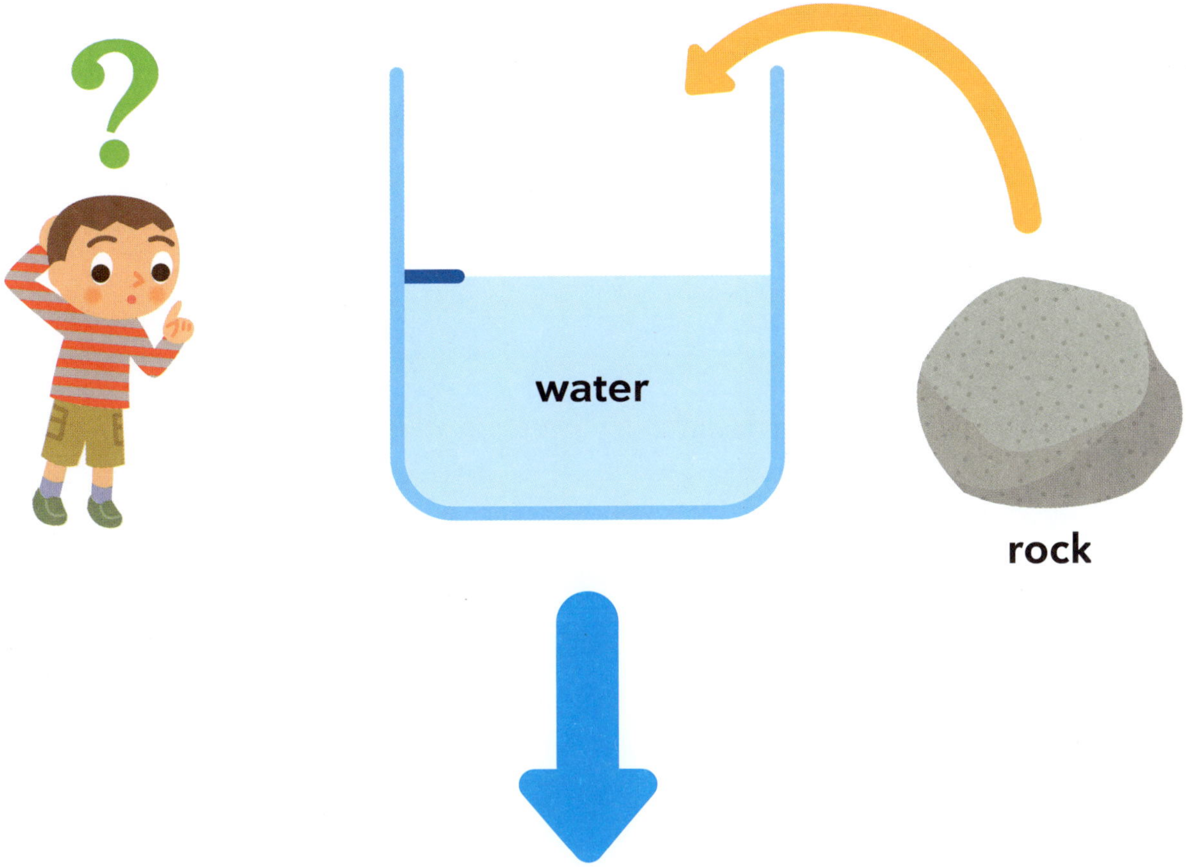

water

rock

(   )   (   )   (   )

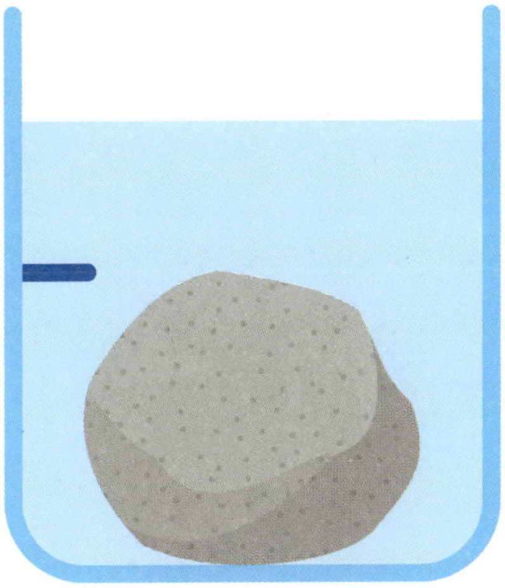

Physical Science

How the Water Line Changes

Adding a marble to the container raises the water level by one mark. Draw a line from ● to ● to show how the water level changes when more marbles are added.

To Parents Putting one marble in the water raises the water level by exactly one mark. Adding two marbles to the water raises it by two marks.

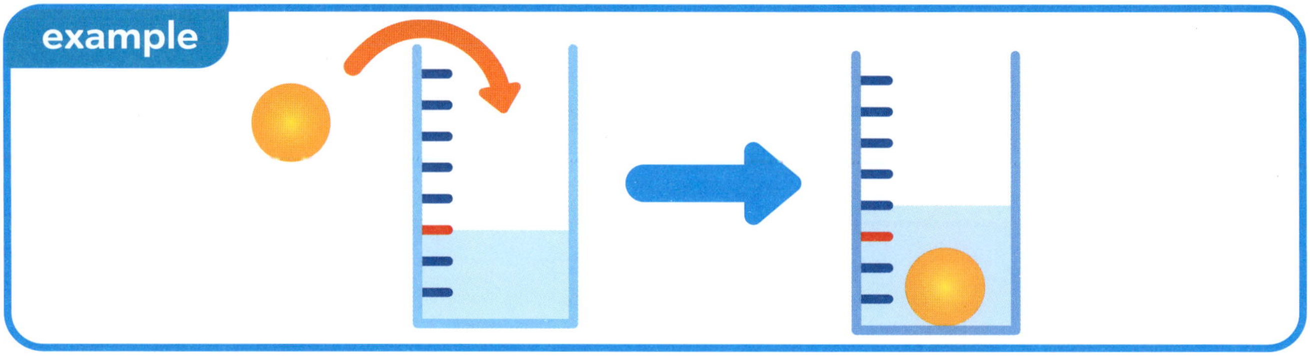

example

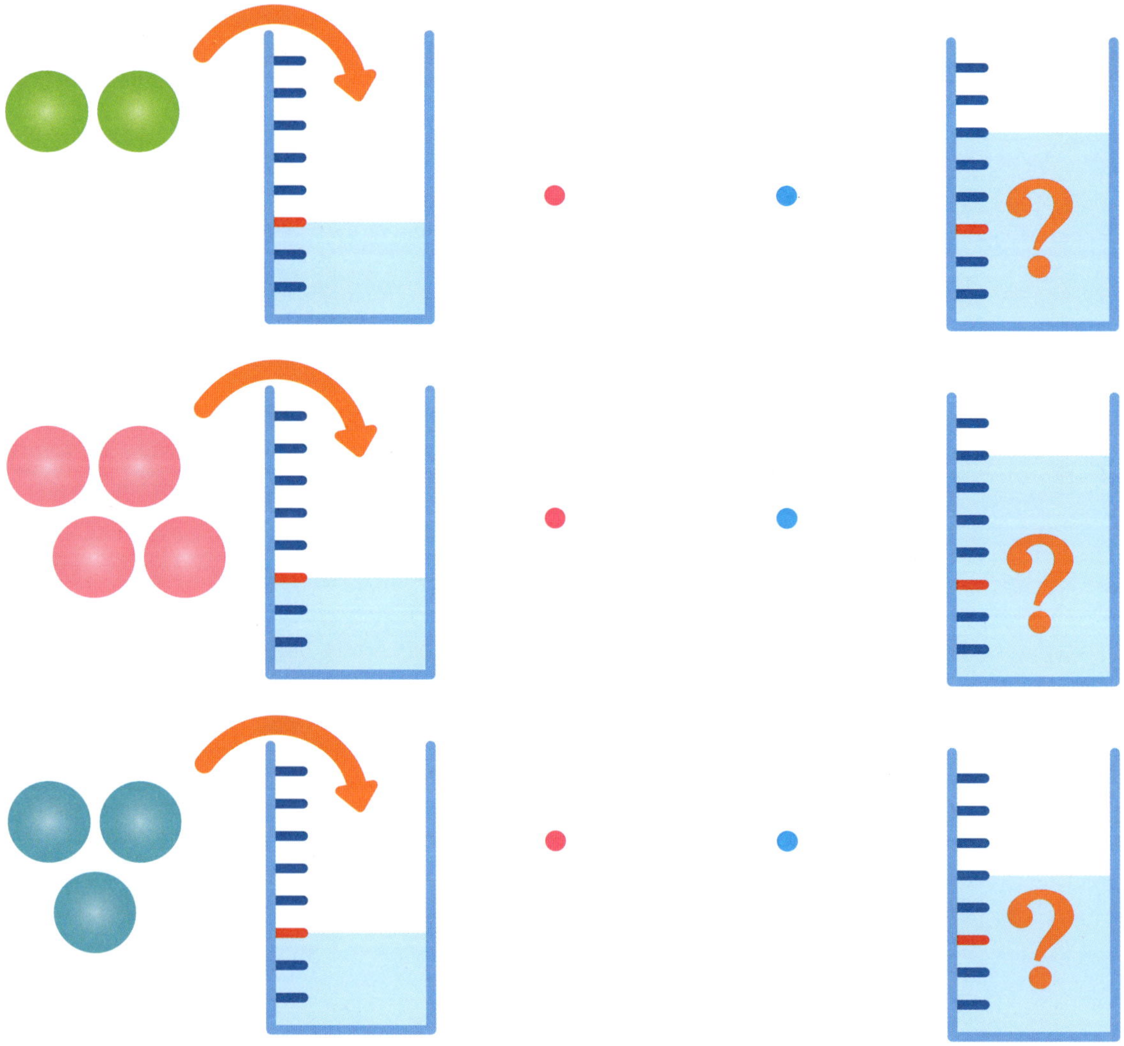

?

?

?

Physical Science

Write the Numbers in Order

Write the numbers 1 to 4 in the ☐ in the order in which the containers would fill up, from fastest to slowest.

To Parents Bigger hoses dispense water more quickly. The more water that comes out in a given time, the less time it takes for the container to fill.

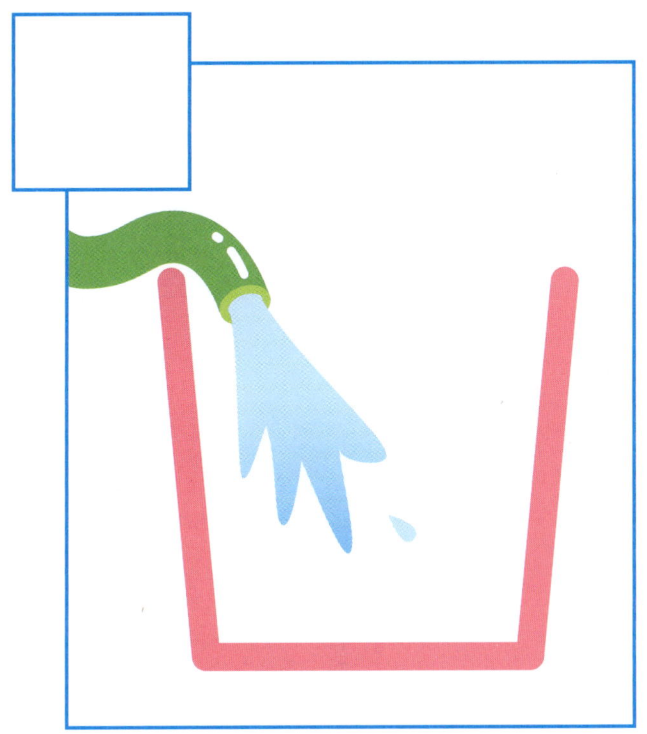

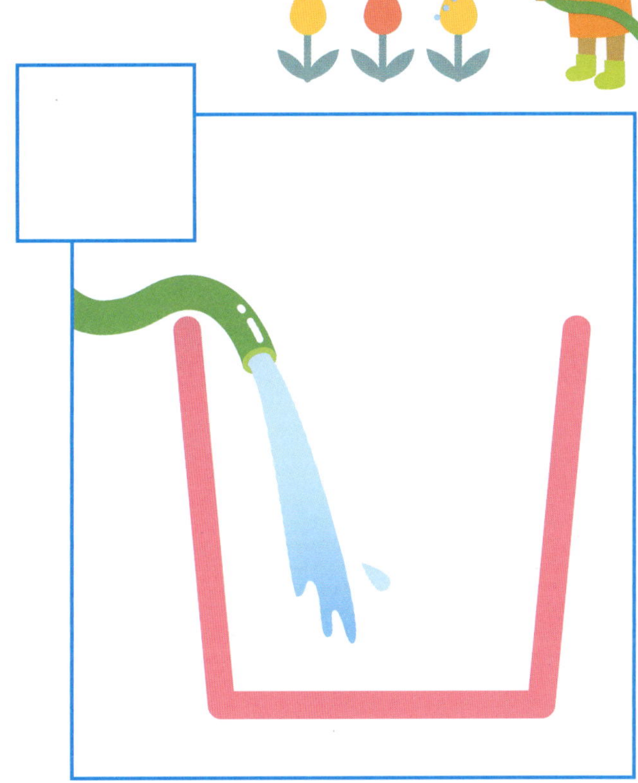

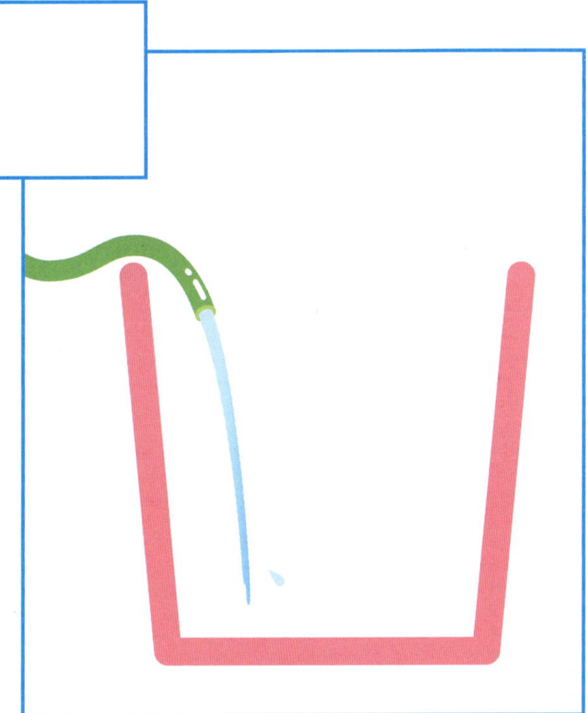

Physical Science

Write the Numbers in Order

Write the numbers 1 to 4 in the ☐ in the order in which the water drains, from fastest to slowest.

To Parents Wider pipes drain water more quickly than thinner pipes. The number of drains and their width affects how quickly the water drains from the pool.

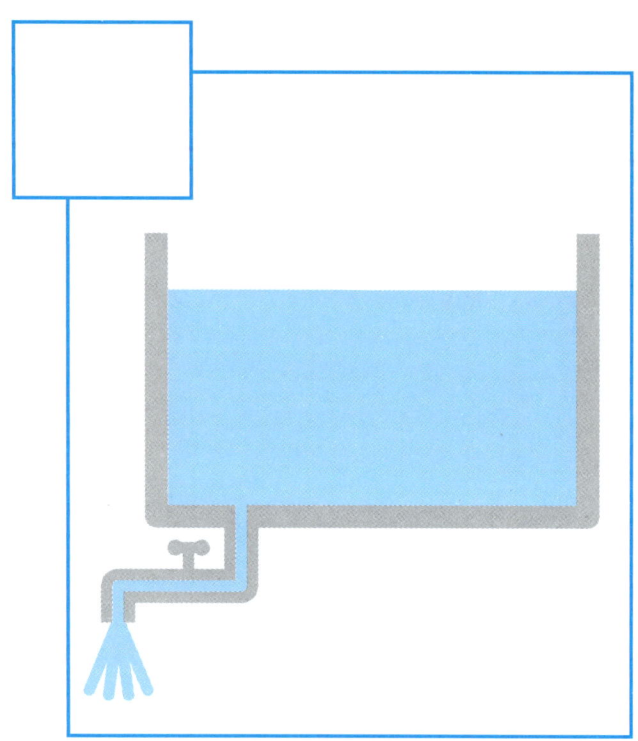

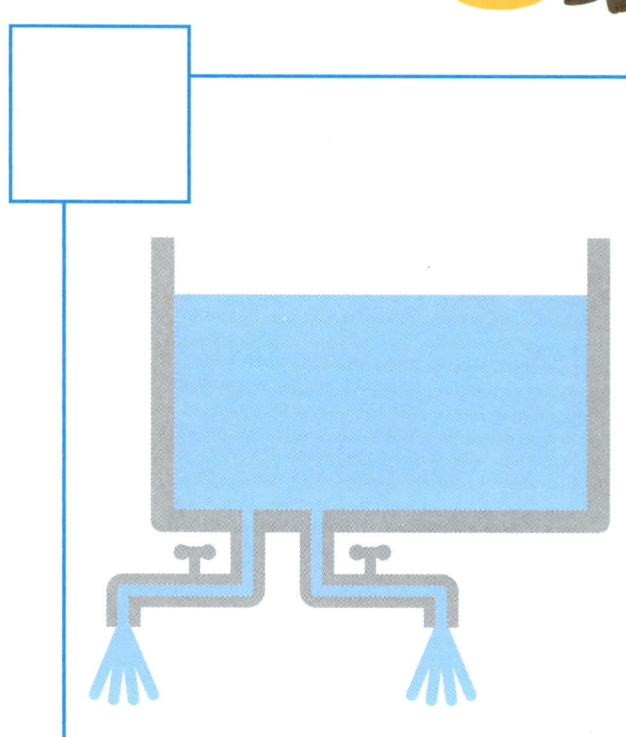

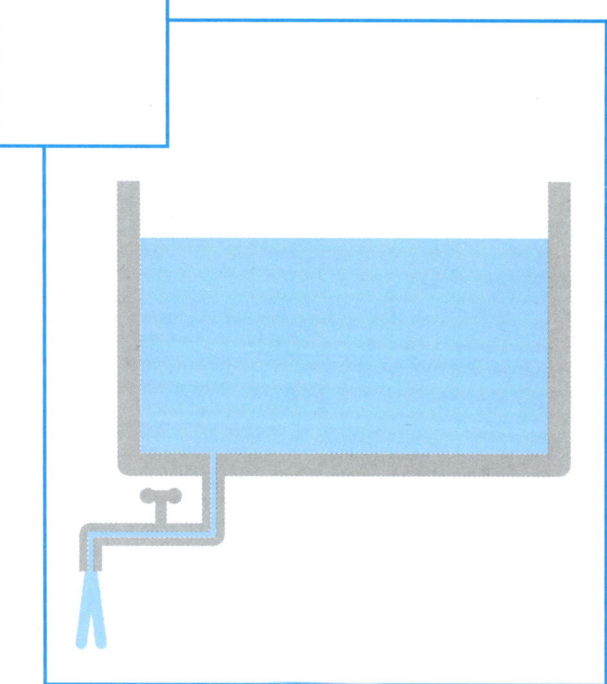

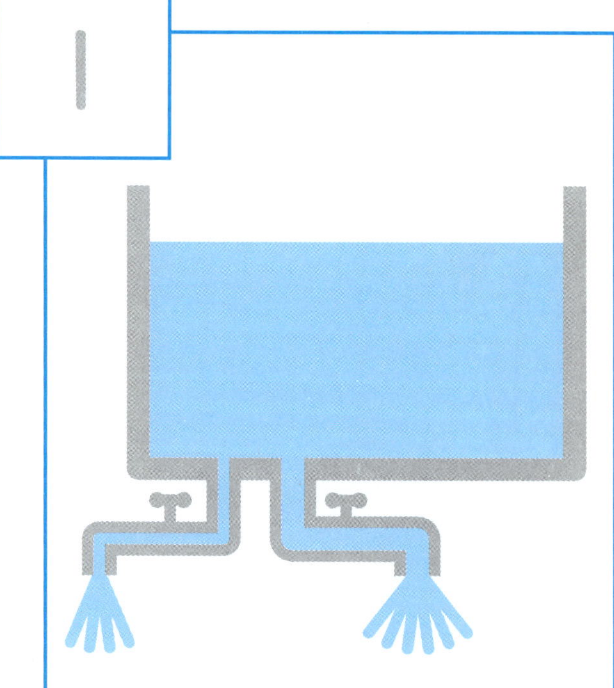

Find the Same Amount

In the example, all of the squares have the same area. Find the pictures below that show the same amount of clay as the example, and draw a ◯ in the (   ) below them.

To Parents In all of the pictures except the bottom one, the clay is divided into four equal parts. The amounts of clay are equal even if the shapes are different.

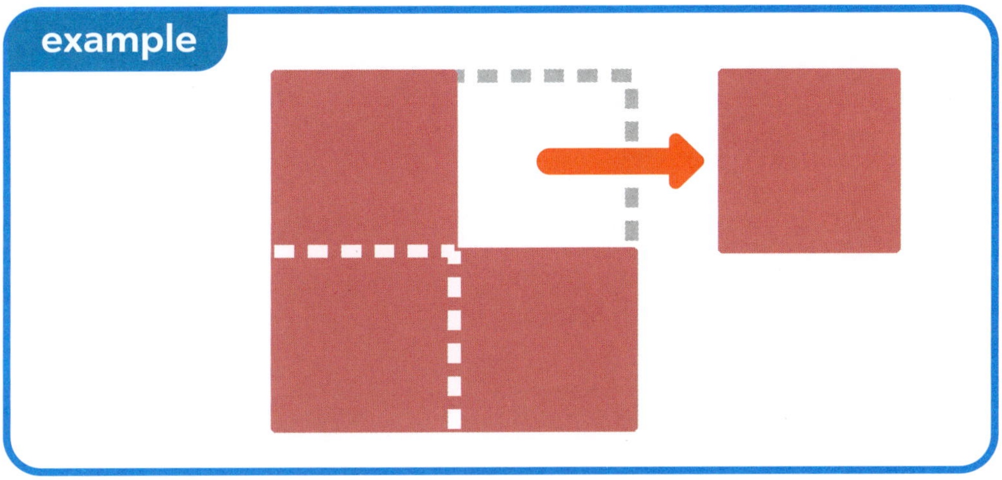

example

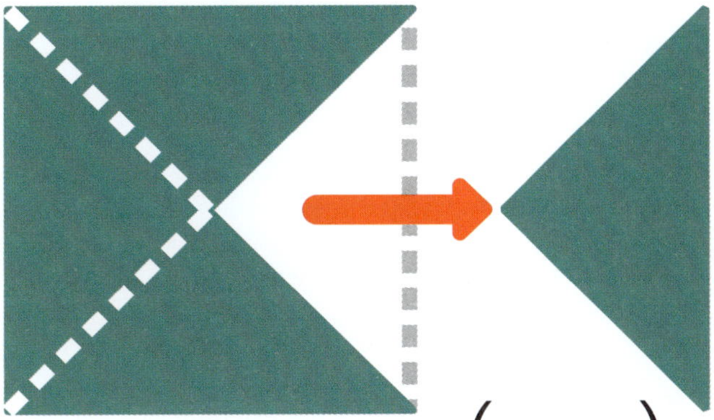

(   )

(   )

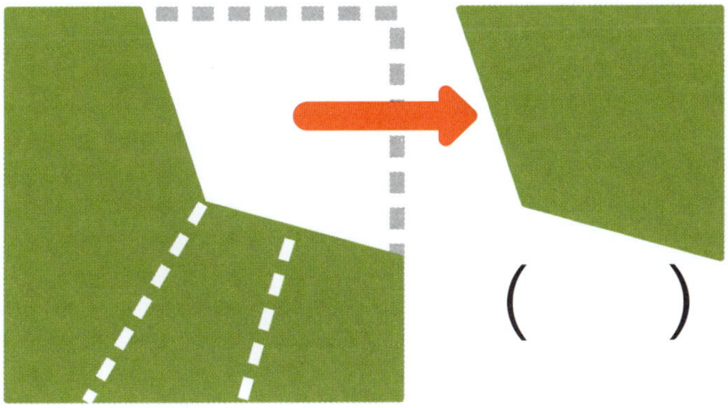

(   )

Find the Same Amount

Two layers of pink clay are cut into different shapes. Find the pictures below that show the same amount of clay as the example, and draw a ◯ in the (   ) next to them.

To Parents The example is two quarters of the sheets of clay. One half is the same size as two quarters.

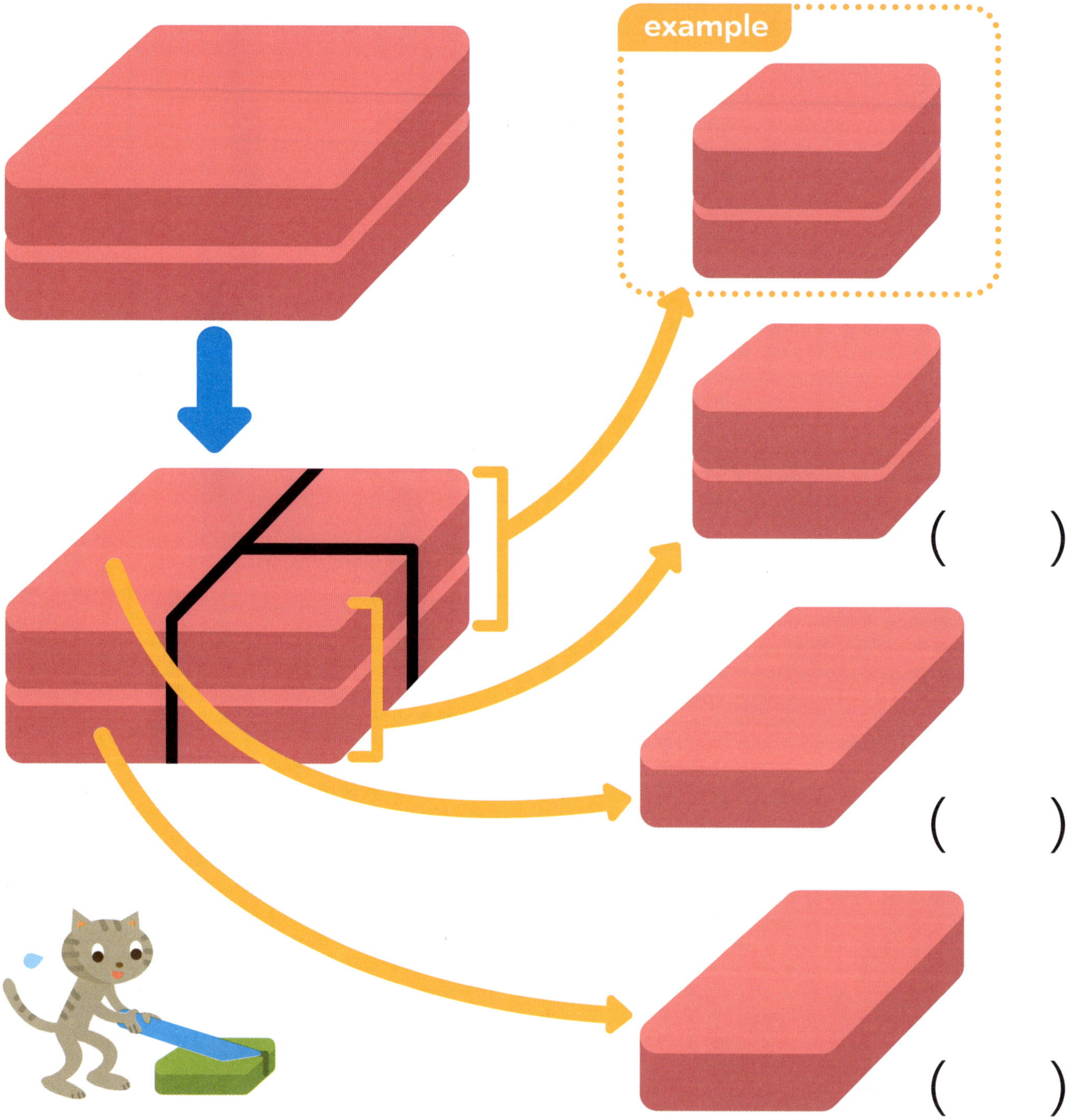

example

(   )

(   )

(   )

Properties of Matter

Which Objects Can Stand Up?

Find objects that can stand up, and draw a ◯ in the ( ) below them.
Try it out with objects around you.

To Parents It is easier for objects to stand up if they are symmetrical and have flat sides. Short objects are less likely to fall over than tall ones, and wide-bottomed objects are less likely to fall over than narrow-bottomed ones.

pencil ( )

penny ( )

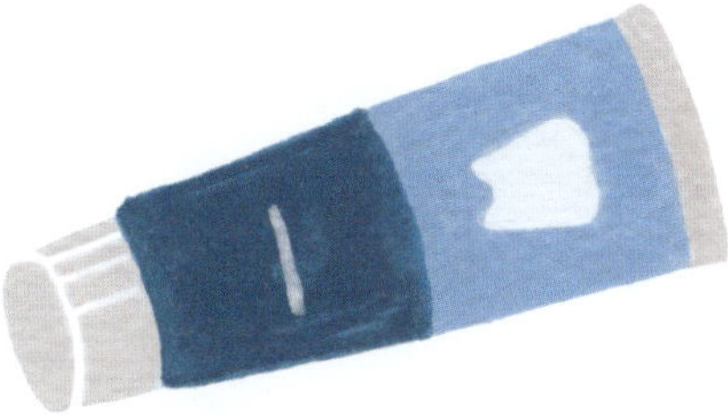

toothpaste ( )

toothbrush ( )

fly swatter ( )

scissors ( )

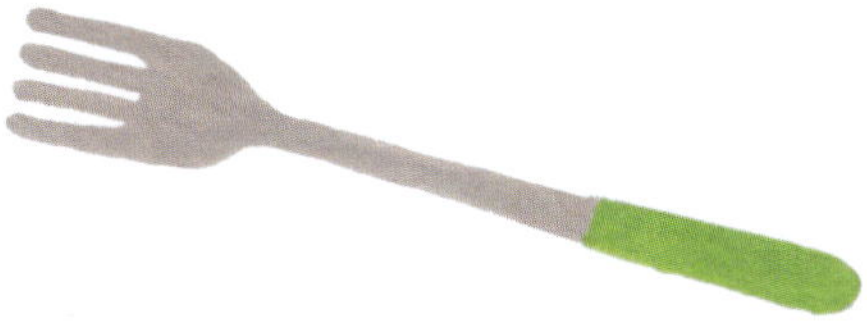

fork ( )

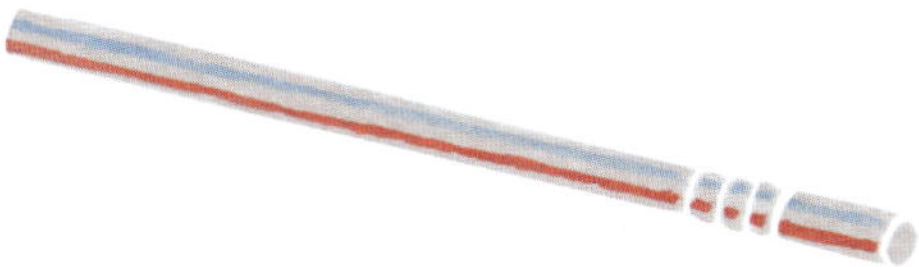

straw ( )

Which Objects Roll Straight?

Find the objects that can roll in a straight line, and draw a ○ in the (   ) below them. Try it out with objects around you.

To Parents Spheres and cylinders can be rolled straight. The texture and hardness of a surface also affect how objects roll.

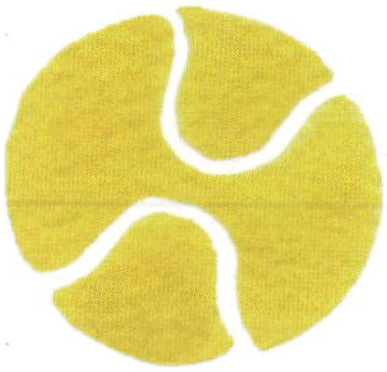

tennis ball
(   )

colored pencil
(   )

lollipop
(   )

can (   )

eraser (   )

candle (   )

wooden toy (   )

cap (   )

Physical Science

Let's Mix Colors

Apply two different colored crayons one after the other, and see what color you get.

To Parents The colors will change depending on the order of the colors you use and how hard you press down on the crayons.

How to Layer Crayon Colors

First apply a thin coat of ① over the entire surface of the drawing. Then, use ② to add another layer of color over ①.

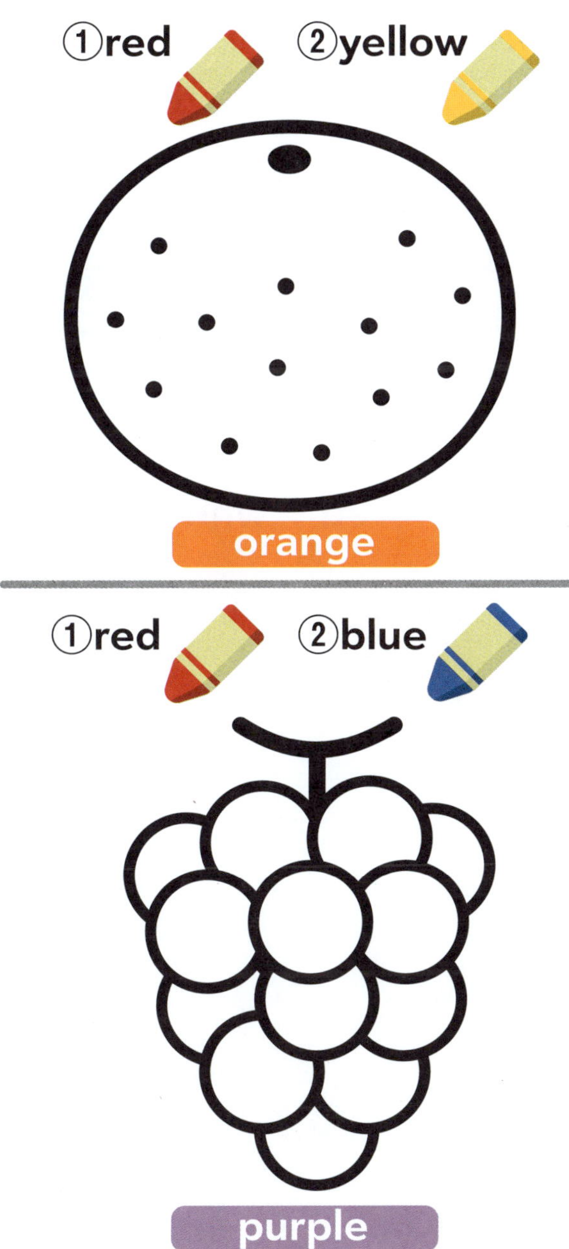

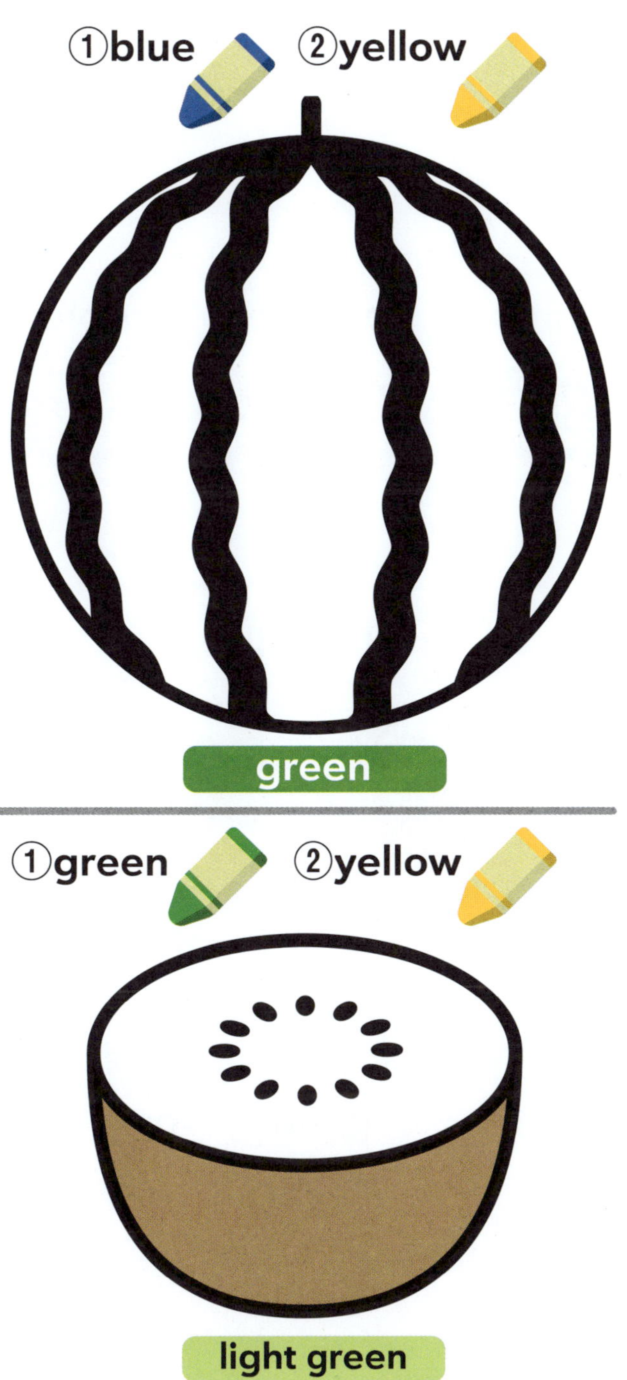

Physical Science

Let's Mix Colors

Find the colors that are created when two crayons are mixed together.
Draw a ◯ in the ( ) below them.

To Parents When a dark blue crayon is mixed with red, it becomes dark bluish purple. When a light blue crayon is mixed with red, it becomes a bright purple.

yellow + blue

green ( ) orange ( ) purple ( )

light blue + red

orange ( ) purple ( ) black ( )

red + yellow

pink ( ) green ( ) orange ( )

red + white

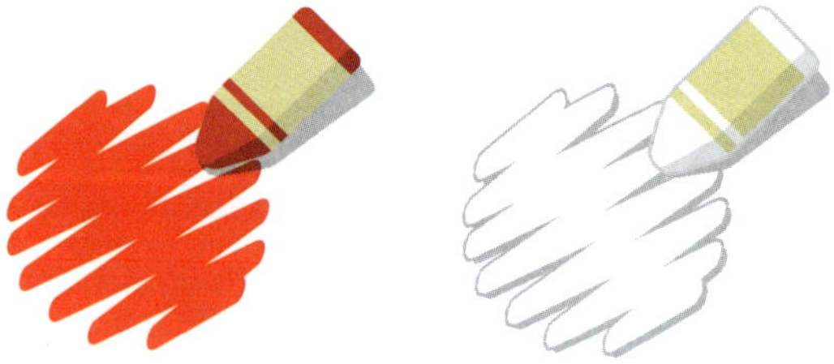

yellow ( ) orange ( ) pink ( )

Which Objects Float?

Find objects that float in water, and draw a ○ in the (   ) next to them.
Try it out with things around you.

To Parents Pencils are made of wood. They float in water because wood is lighter than water. Paper clips are made of metal and sink because metal is denser than water.

marble  (   ) pencil (   ) plastic bottle (   )

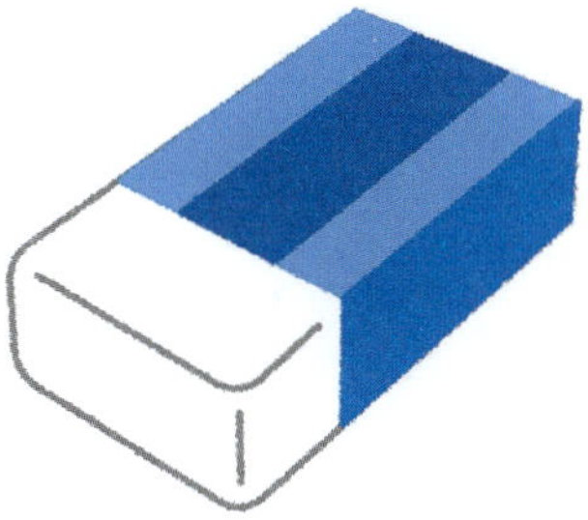

eraser 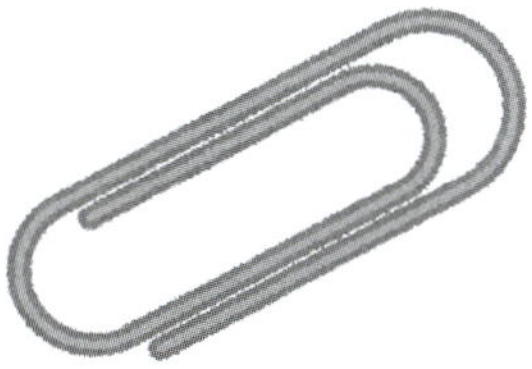 (   ) paper clip  (   ) toothpick (   )

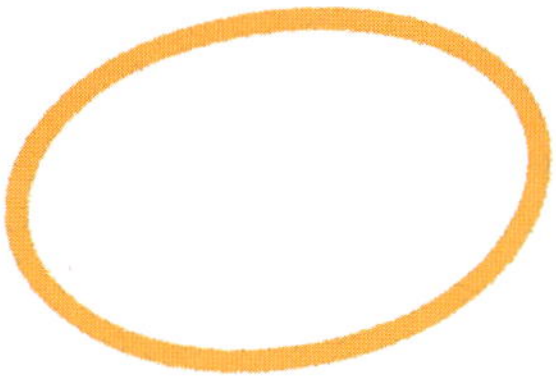

rubber band 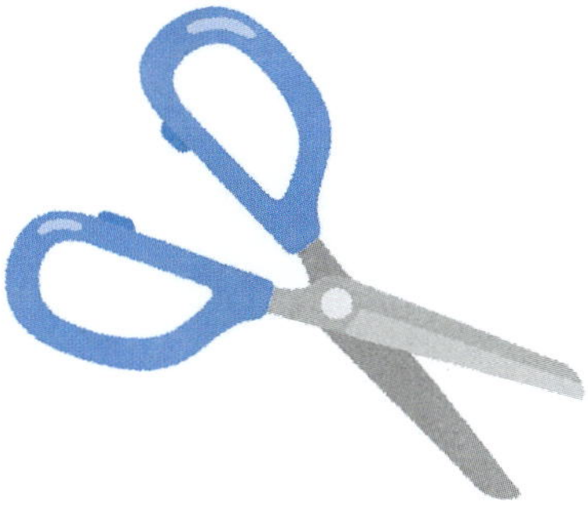 (   ) scissors 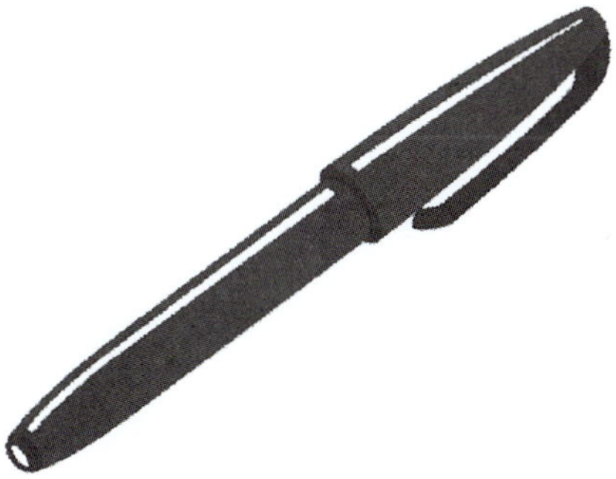 (   ) felt tip pen (   )

Which Fruits Float?

Find the fruits that float in water, and draw a ○ in the (　) below them. Try it out with fruits around you.

To Parents Fruits with a high sugar content are denser because they contain more sugar. Their higher density makes them heavier, so they sink more easily in water than less sugary fruits that are the same size.

apple

(　　)

kiwifruit

(　　)

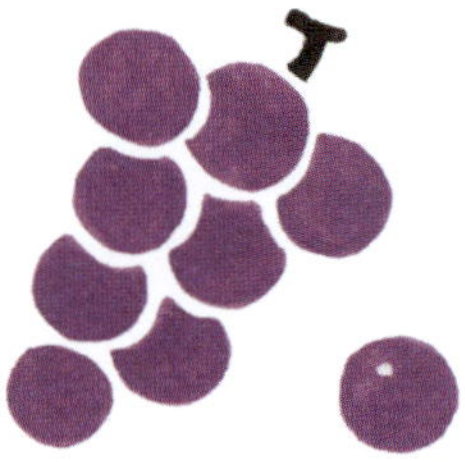

grape

(　　)

mandarin orange

(　　)

banana

(　　)

Which Objects Stick to Magnets?

Find the objects that stick to magnets, and draw a ◯ in the (   ) below them.

To Parents Iron, cobalt, and nickel are attracted to magnets. A penny is made mostly of zinc and is not attracted to magnets.

magnet

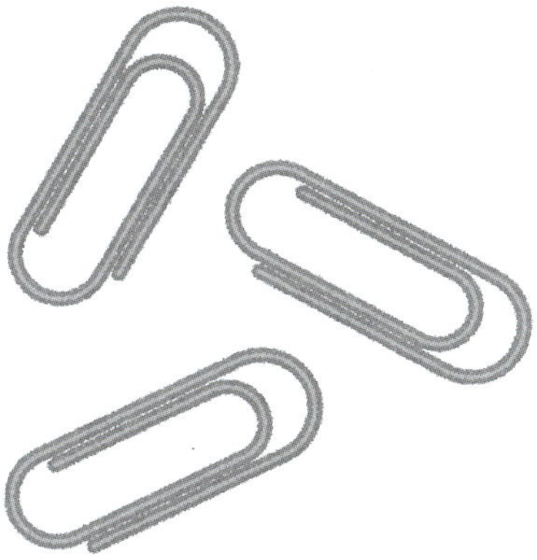

---

paper clip (   )

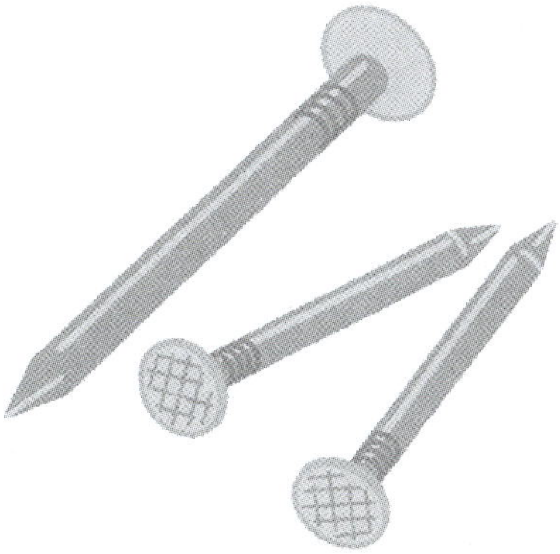

iron nail (   )

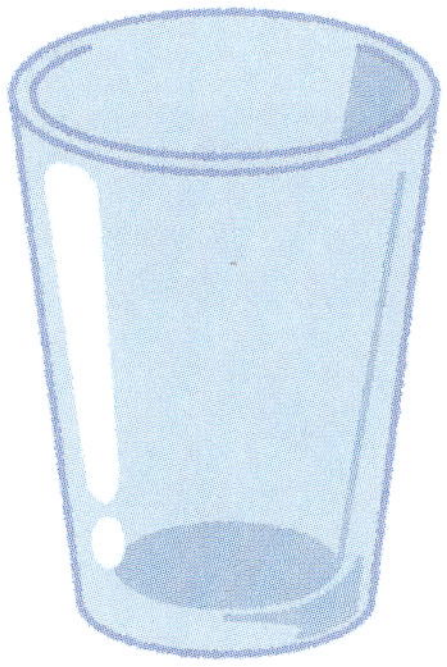

glass (   )

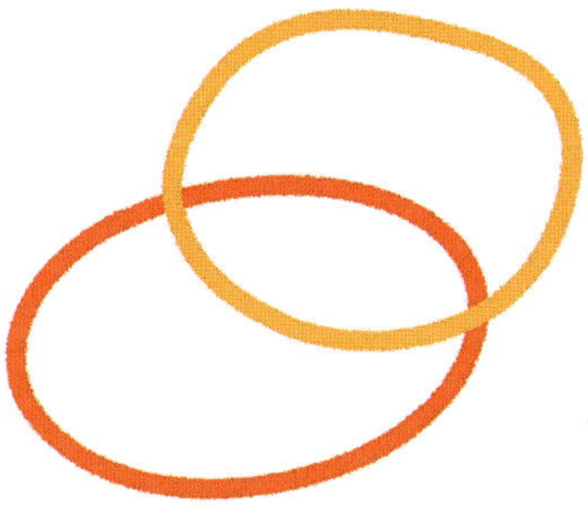

rubber band (   )

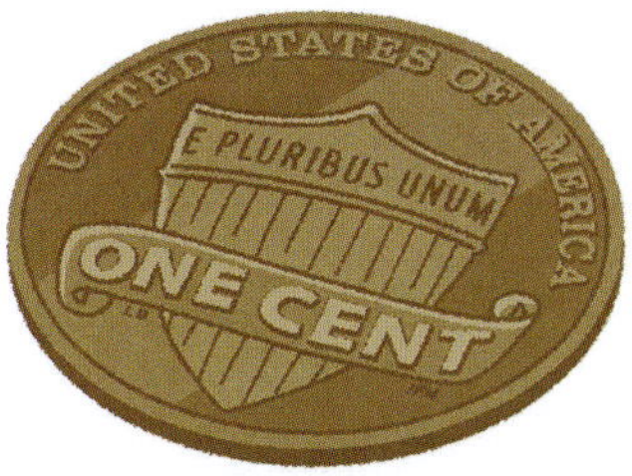

penny (   )

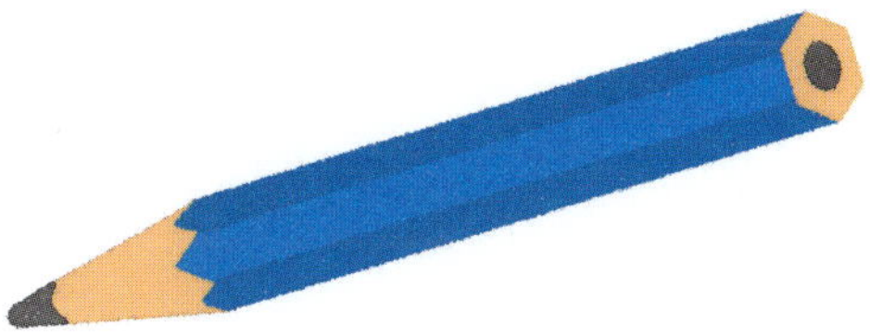

pencil (   )

Let's Experiment with Magnets

Find two pictures where the relationship between the magnet and the paper clips is incorrect, and draw an X in the (   ) below them. Use actual magnets and paper clips to find the mistakes.

To Parents The two ends of the magnet are the north and south poles, where the magnetic force is strongest.

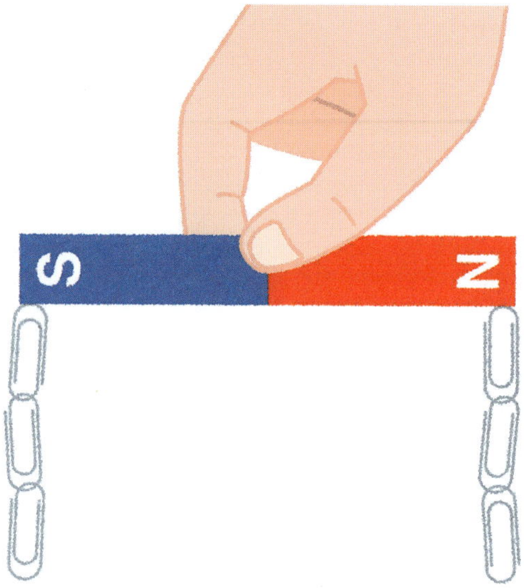

(   ) (   )

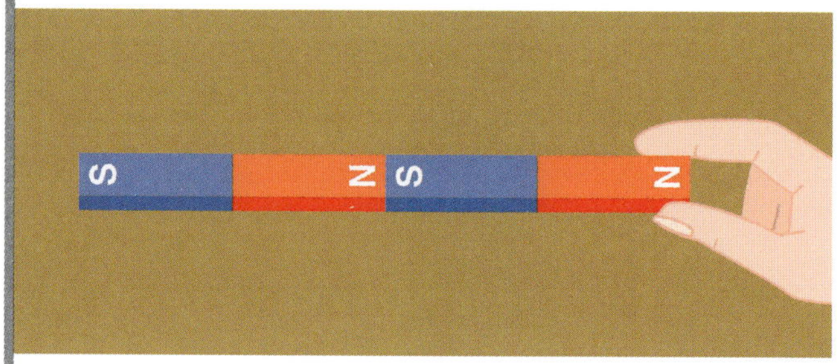

(   ) (   )

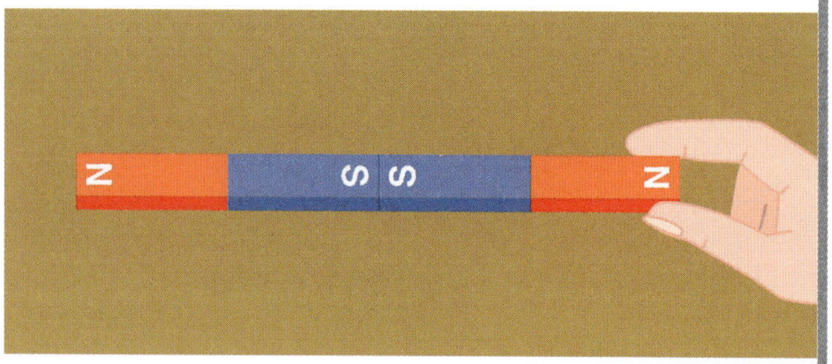

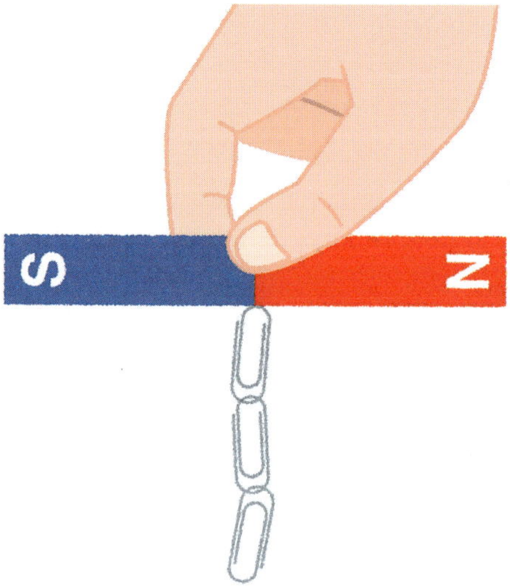

Physical Science

Look at a Picture Through a Glass

Look at the picture of the teddy bear through a glass of water. See how the image of the picture in the water changes with the distance between the cup and the picture. Put a sticker on the matching position of the picture and the glass.

To Parents When the glass is close to the picture, it acts like a magnifying glass, and when it's far away, it functions like a camera lens. Try it for yourself. Make sure to use a glass with a smooth surface.

When the distance to the glass is close

When the distance to the glass is far away

sticker

sticker

Physical Science

Make a Straw Mobile

Tie a string around the center of a straw. Hang two objects of the different size and shape from each side of the straw and test its balance. Place stickers below to show when the straw is balanced and when it is out of balance.

To Parents Heavier objects or those hung further from the pivot point will have a greater effect on the balance of the mobile. Tie the string at the center of the straw to ensure it balances horizontally.

How the straw looks when it is out of balance	How the straw looks when it is balanced
sticker	sticker

Answer Key

1
apple
orange
apricot
2
apple
kiwifruit
cherry
apricot
lemon
3
apple
orange
apricot
pineapple
4
kiwifruit
banana
cantaloupe
strawberry
5
watermelon
cantaloupe
6
eggplant
cucumber
avocado
okra
7
tomato
cabbage
8
corn
pea
peanut
9
sunflower
morning glory
tomato
rose
10
1
2
4
3
11
dandelion
tulip
carnation
sunflower
12
rose clover
rose
daisy
lily
13
lily
brassica
hibiscus
dandelion
14
tomato
eggplant
green pepper
cucumber
pumpkin
watermelon
15
Some vegetables are the leafy parts of a plant.
cabbage
arugula
spinach
Some vegetables are the root part of a plant.
carrot
parsnip
radish
Some vegetables are the flower part of a plant.
cauliflower
broccoli
artichoke
16
1
4
3
2
17
beaver
octopus
black-capped chickadee
oriental longheaded locust
sea
grassy field
lake
woods
18
starfish
squid
salmon
salamander
crab
sea urchin
sea anemone
frog
19
owl
bat
penguin
flying squirrel
chicken
ostrich
20
shark
flying fish
dolphins
tuna
whale

21
frog
rabbit
sea lion
monkey
22
kangaroo
bear
elephant
horse
23
panda
polar bear
pig
rabbit
24
koala
elephant
fox
mouse
25
horse
cow
pig
fox
26
kangaroo
squirrel
mouse
lion
27
grasshopper
praying mantis
cicada
dragonfly
28
ladybug
butterfly
ant
bee
29
lion
wild boar
deer
malayan tapir
30
raccoon
bear
panda
hedgehog
31
frog
ostrich
chicken
sea turtle
herring
32
1
3
4
2
33
34
35
diplodocus
lizard
triceratops
rhinoceros
tyrannosaurus
stegosaurus
bat
saber-toothed tiger
36
37
Direction of the wind
38
39
2
4
3
1
40

41
42
43
44
45
46
close
far
close
far
47
48
49
50
51
iron
kettle
wind-up toy
music box
TV
wood stove
lantern
52
car
rowboat
bicycle
skateboard
tricycle
motorcycle
53
sparrow (3)
plane (1)
butterfly (4)
paraglider (2)
a single pearl (4)
baseball (2)
a piece of candy (3)
soccer ball (1)
54
watermelon (4)
egg (2)
cherry (1)
baseball (3)
doughnut (2)
DVD (3)
penny (1)
pool float (4)
55
(2)
(3)
(1)
56
lemon
honey
Black tea is made from young leaves.
young leaves
black tea
57
3 2 1 4
58
grass
concrete
grass
4 2 1 3
59
60

61
water
rock
62
example
63
64
65
example
66
example
67
pencil
penny
toothpaste
toothbrush
fly swatter
scissors
fork
straw
68
tennis ball
colored pencil
lollipop
can
eraser
candle
wooden toy
cap
69
How to Layer Crayon Colors
①blue ②yellow
①red ②yellow
orange
green
①red ②blue
①green ②yellow
purple
light green
70
yellow + blue
light blue + red
green orange purple
orange purple black
red + yellow
red + white
pink green orange
yellow orange pink
71
marble
pencil
plastic bottle
eraser
paper clip
toothpick
rubber band
scissors
felt tip pen
72
apple
kiwifruit
grape
mandarin orange
banana
73
magnet
paper clip
iron nail
glass
rubber band
penny
pencil
74
75
When the distance to the glass is close
When the distance to the glass is far away
76
How the straw looks when it is out of balance
How the straw looks when it is balanced